Year of Awesome!
How You Can Use 12 Success Principles including *10 Seconds to Wealth*

*10th Anniversary Edition
reimagined and revised*

Tom Marcoux

Executive Coach

Spoken Word Strategist

Speaker-Author of 40 books

Blogger, YourBodySoulandProsperity.com

A QuickBreakthrough Publishing Edition

Copyright © 2016 Tom Marcoux Media, LLC
ISBN-13: 978-0997809831
ISBN-10: 0997809833

10th Anniversary Edition, reimagined and revised

All rights reserved. No part of this book may be reproduced or transmitted in any form by any means electronic or mechanical, including photocopying, recording or by any information storage and retrieval system without written permission from the publisher.

QuickBreakthrough Publishing is an imprint of Tom Marcoux Media, LLC. More copies are available from the publisher, Tom Marcoux Media, LLC. Please write TomSuperCoach@gmail.com

or visit www.TomSuperCoach.com

or Tom's blog: www.BeHeardandBeTrusted.com

This book was developed and written with care. Names and details were modified to respect privacy.

Disclaimer: The author and publisher acknowledge that each person's situation is unique, and that readers have full responsibility to seek consultations with health, financial, spiritual and legal professionals. The author and publisher make no representations or warranties of any kind, and the author and publisher shall not be liable for any special, consequential or exemplary damages resulting, in whole or in part, from the reader's use of, or reliance upon, this material.:

Other Books by Tom Marcoux:
- What the Rich Don't Say about Getting Rich
- Shine! Don't Let Toxic People Extinguish Your Dreams
- Soar! Nothing Can Stop You This Year
- Time Management Secrets the Rich Won't Tell You
- Discover Your Enchanted Prosperity
- Emotion-Motion Life Hacks … for More Success and Happiness
- Relax Your Way Networking
- Connect: High Trust Communication for Your Success
- Darkest Secrets of Persuasion and Seduction Masters
- Darkest Secrets of Charisma
- Darkest Secrets of Negotiation Masters
- Darkest Secrets of Making a Pitch to the Film / TV Industry

Praise for *Year of Awesome!* and Tom Marcoux
• "Tom Marcoux's *Year of Awesome!* focuses on how each of us have divine gifts that we need to understand and use to be our best when those crucial 10 seconds occur. Tom includes hard data research from neuroscience ... He identifies the divine gifts and throughout the book shares how these gifts can help us create what we want in our lives, and the wealth we want. He brings his vast experience with clients and real world situations to the book, sharing secrets with the reader on how he helped others." – Linda Finkle, author of *Finding The Fork In The Road: The Art of Maximizing the Potential of Business Partnerships*
• "I like the premise of this book that you can create wealth in only 10 seconds. That's because wealth is created in the mind. ... A negative event can be permanently fixed in the brain in an instant. But it takes a positive thought 10 seconds to become indelibly encoded in the brain. Tom Marcoux has distinguished himself as a coach, speaker and self-help author. The book contains practical and spiritual ways for you to increase your abundance. Increase your confidence, which is essential to success in any business or personal endeavor. Learn the power of teamwork and the essential element of action, among other valuable insights." – Danek S. Kaus, co-author, *Power Persuasion*

Praise for Tom Marcoux's Other Work:
• "Concerned about networking situations? Get *Relax Your Way Networking*. Success is built on high trust relationships. Master Coach Tom Marcoux reveals secrets to increase your influence."
– Greg S. Reid, Author, *Think and Grow Rich Series*
• "In Tom Marcoux's *Now You See Me*, the powerful and easy-to-use ideas can make a big difference in your business and your personal relationships." – Allen Klein, author of *You Can't Ruin My Day*
• "In *Darkest Secrets of Persuasion and Seduction Masters: How to Protect Yourself and Turn the Power to Good*, learn useful countermeasures to protect you from being darkly manipulated."
– David Barron, co-author, *Power Persuasion*
• "In *Connect*, Tom's advice on how to remain true to yourself and establish authentic rapport with clients is both insightful and reality based. He [shows how] to establish oneself as a credible expert."
- Arthur P. Ciaramicoli, Ed.D., Ph.D., author *The Curse of the Capable*
• "In *Reduce Clutter, Enlarge Your Life*, Marcoux will help you get rid of the physical and mental clutter occupying precious space in your life. You'll reclaim wasted energy, lower your stress, and find time for new opportunities." – Laura Stack, author of *Execution IS the Strategy*
Visit Tom's blog: www.YourBody Soul and Prosperity.com

Tom Marcoux

CONTENTS

Dedication and Acknowledgments	6
Book One: Your *Year of Awesome!*	7
Connect with Your *Divine Gifts*	9
9-Minute Miracle Breakthrough and your Momentum Action Plan (MAP)	45
The Power of *10 Seconds to Wealth*	76
Articles are interspersed in this book . . . by guest authors Mike Robbins, Dr. Elayne Savage and Dr. Arthur P. Ciaramicoli	
Create Warm Relationships; Prosperity is Built on Good Relationships	89
Book Two: 10 Seconds to Wealth—Additional Topics	151
Book Three: 10 Seconds to Wealth—More Topics	159
Book Four: Prepare Yourself to Be Strong for the Unknowns	167
Final Word; Excerpt from *Darkest Secrets of Persuasion and Seduction Masters: How to Protect Yourself and Turn the Power to Good*	191,192
Special Offer Just for Readers, About the Author Tom Marcoux	191,198

DEDICATION AND ACKNOWLEDGEMENTS

This book is dedicated to the terrific book and film consultant, and author Johanna E. Mac Leod. It is also dedicated to the other team members. Thanks to Barry Adamson II for editing new sections of this book. Thanks to Linda L. Chappo, Stacy Diane Horn and Jill Ronsley (SunEditWrite.com) for editing other portions of this book.

Thanks to guest authors Mike Robbins, Dr. Elayne Savage and Dr. Arthur P. Ciaramicoli. [Their articles remain with their original copyright and are included in this book by their permission.]

Thanks to Gregg at kunst+aventur for his work on a previous version of this book. Thanks to my father, Al Marcoux, for his concern and efforts for me. Thanks to my mother, Sumiyo Marcoux, a kind, generous soul. Thank you to Higher Power. Thanks to our readers, audiences, clients, my graduate/college students and my team members of Tom Marcoux Media, LLC. The best to you.

Book One:
Your *Year of Awesome!*

Imagine that you can have what you truly want. How? When you unwrap your divine gifts for success, love and great relationships.

Through this book you'll learn to unwrap your Divine Gifts and experience the process of *10 Seconds to Wealth*.

Now, in this 10th Anniversary edition of this book, fully reimagined and revised, it is a joy to share with you both practical and spiritual methods to uplift your life.

As an Executive Coach and the Spoken Word Strategist, I work with CEOs, business owners and managers. In a session, I emphasize: "I'm in the business of *transformation*. I'm *not* in the business of Band-Aids. I'm not your employee. I'm not a friend afraid of rocking a friendship. I'll help you see *what you need to see* so you get what YOU want. That's my agenda. That my purpose."

Through this book, I am now acting as *your* Executive Coach.

What do you really want? Let's take action to make that

happen!

In this book, I share *12 Success Principles* as embodied in the S.U.C.C.E.S.S.-A.C.T.-N.O.W. process.

This book is divided into 12 Sections based on 12 months of the year. Let's take a look at the 12 Principles:

S.U.C.C.E.S.S.-A.C.T.-N.O.W.
1. S – share in your Divine Gifts
2. U – uplift through "the most important"
3. C – concentrate on Top Six Targets
4. C – create your "reserves"
5. E – energize "10 Seconds to Wealth"
6. S – succeed through commitment to "the pipeline and better-than-zero"
7. S – sort and Declare a New Chapter of Life
8. A – act to support friendships
9. C – continue learning
10. T – target "act it until you become it"
11. N – nurture gratitude
12. O – open with "the sacred"
BONUS: W – win by listening

In various sections of this book, I refer to "10 Seconds to Wealth" which relates to a) in 10 seconds one can improve a relationship, close a sale and more; and b) the brain requires 10 seconds of focused attention so that something *positive* can go into one's long-term memory. An extended discussion of *10 Seconds to Wealth* appears in the "May" section of this book.

Let's move forward …

January – New Beginnings

How do you feel about a new year? Do you look upon it as a time of new beginnings?

Or do you, on some level, seek to protect yourself from experiencing some form of disappointment? Many of us protect ourselves by avoiding New Year's Resolutions.

It's reported that 50% of those who start an exercise program drop out within the first six months (a 2009 study in the *International Journal of Sport and Exercise Psychology*).

I've learned that it takes strategy to permanently install new habits. Fortunately, one day I discovered something that provides *an edge* in terms of improving our lives.

My Epiphany

While teaching a Comparative Religion class, I wrote these details on a whiteboard:

Existential Plights
Death, Freedom, Responsibility, Meaninglessness**

[** The Existential Plights are discussed in the classic book *Existential Psychotherapy* by Irvin D. Yalom.]

By the mere fact that you're a human being, it is said that you are stuck with the Existential Plights.

I then did something new in the class. I wrote on the other side of the whiteboard:

Divine Gifts
Love, Humility, Forgiveness, Faith, Grace, Art

In that moment, standing at the whiteboard, I was struck with the idea: *These Divine Gifts provide healing as we're faced with the Existential Plights.* How about that!

Now we're going to explore how you can tune into your Divine Gifts and open the floodgates for wealth, financial abundance and warm relationships. We'll use the

D.I.V.I.N.E. process.
1. Decide (love)
2. Intuit (humility)
3. Voice (forgiveness)
4. Inspire (faith)
5. Nurture (grace)
6. Express (art)

Through this book you'll learn how to experience your Divine Gifts. To obtain the best results, you will need to actively prepare. The next section on love, humility, forgiveness, faith, grace and art is a springboard to condition your brain for more wealth. For the sake of our discussion, we'll hold that wealth includes financial abundance, good relationships and feelings of fulfillment and well-being.

The New Beginning we're talking about here is to move forward from this moment onward with a new understanding of your Divine Gifts.

We'll begin with this principle for your *Year of Awesome*:
Principle #1: Share in your Divine Gifts.

When I say "share in" I mean, picture that your Divine Gifts are a feast that you want to enjoy. It's up to you to become active and really experience the blessings of your Divine Gifts.

****

A Note about Your Divine Gifts and Relief Related to the Existential Plights

The Existential Plights of death, freedom, responsibility and meaninglessness basically give each person an off-balance feeling often called "free-floating anxiety," which is defined as a generalized and persistent fear that is not attributable to anything specific. The following gives an example for each Existential Plight:

Anxiety about death is often felt in the moment as fear for something that is going dreadfully wrong. It can be the fear of saying something wrong or even losing a sale.

People who are afraid of making a wrong decision may feel that their freedom of choice is a burden.

Many people equate responsibility with the burden of blame. On the subconscious level, this can be manifested as an echo of parental admonishments: "You need to be more responsible!" and "You're to blame for this going wrong!"

Meaninglessness can be the burden of feeling "groundless." This happens when one feels disillusioned. Perhaps one feels betrayed by a parent or friend. Perhaps following a spiritual path didn't provide long-lasting comfort.

The blessings and power of the Divine Gifts are that they give us uplifting support in the moment. The Divine Gifts of love, humility, forgiveness, faith, grace and art give you the experience of fullness, which is the opposite of emptiness or vulnerability.

* * * * * *

Decide (love)

When have you really felt loved? Did someone give you a gift? Or hug you when you were crying?

Now come with me on a brief journey, which may become a real shift in your thoughts and feelings.

Imagine that you and I stand and say plaintively: "I need love." Do you feel emptiness in your chest? A hole that needs to be filled up? Some people feel the discomfort of "I need love" to be similar to that of overwhelming heat in a desert.

Imagine that you're in a desert feeling stifled by the weather and you're perspiring. Then, a delicious, cool breeze comes along and embraces you. Now you feel relieved and comfortable. Ahhh. You pick up a cool glass of water with ice cubes and take a drink. Ahhh.

Can you imagine that great feeling of relief? It's similar to the relief we feel when we truly experience "I am love."

The state of being when you deeply feel "I am love" is one of comfort, joy, faith and happiness.

My goal with this section is to introduce you (or perhaps remind you) to an essential distinction. Why? So you'll feel better and stronger.

Ready?

Imagine you have a ruler. On the left side is "I need love." On the right side is "I am love."

I ask you: Which of these two sides feels stronger?

Now imagine two cars. (For the sake of this conversation, both cars run on electric batteries.) The car with a fully charged battery can get up and go! The car without the charge is powerless. It's stuck. It's empty.

When you say "I am love," you are fully charged. You have power. Even better than that, saying "I am love" means to many of us that a person is one with a supportive Higher Power.

Love is a Divine Gift.

You, as a human being, have the ability to love as "standard equipment." This is not to say that it's always easy to be loving. It is a moment-to-moment decision.

To get to that "I am love" part of your being is to make a decision.

What decision?

Often, it is to let your first reflex thought (often a judgment) flow by. Instead, find a compassionate thought and action.

Use compassion as your compass.

What does this look like?

You choose loving actions:

1. Restrain yourself from writing an angry letter to a rude relative.
2. Give a surprise gift to a friend to help her feel important.
3. Listen to the same story for the tenth time when an elderly relative tells it.

When you use "I am love" and "compassion as your compass," you can enhance your personal relationships.

Use love & compassion to open the floodgates of wealth

When you work with customers (or a supervisor or coworkers), make each *10 Seconds to Wealth** count. How? Enter each moment with "I am love." You do that by finding a way to express compassion. In particular, notice that there are two (often unvoiced) requirements that your customers hold: a) Show me that I can trust you, and b) Make me feel important.

When you fulfill those two requirements, customers will purchase more and refer new business back to you.

People often spend more for the services that they trust. For example, I have paid for about 18 domain names over the years, although I do not use the cheapest provider. Why? Because I seek reliability. I use two companies that have served me well. I have no complaints with either of them. Neither gives me hassles or reason for concern.

Opportunities often come from people who like and trust you.

So it all comes down to one idea:

Start from a place of "I am love." That's right. Make a decision and then act on it.

* We'll discuss more about *10 Seconds to Wealth* in the "May" section of this book

And guess what! You start to feel better and you start to feel safer. Why? Because you are now aligned with the good in the Universe.

You are empowered. You are loved.

Remember to focus on "I am love."

Principle: Embrace the idea "I am love."

Power Questions: Are you ready to enter each situation from a base of "I am love"? Will you look at situations using compassion as your compass?

* * * * * *

Intuit (humility)

Do you have a friend who seems to make life more of a struggle than necessary? Have you noticed that he or she likes complaining? Such a person is often inflexible.

But that's *not* you or me. Right?

Life has given me a number of opportunities to learn about something I call "healthy humility."

Healthy humility is a great alternative to being inflexible and holding onto some preconceived notion about how things are supposed to be.

Instead, I've learned to take a flexible stance and flow with life instead of allowing reflexive judgments to cloud my thinking.

How? Let's say I find it rude that a relative won't take my phone calls. I let my initial thoughts flow by. I focus on:

- I wonder what I can learn here.
- Maybe this person is not skilled at handling upset feelings.
- What would I rather think about?

The rigid stance of insisting that other people should do something can block the flow of your intuition. How? Because nothing new can get in. Your intuition gives you the gift of new ideas.

Your intuition can give you new solutions that are more expansive than mere rational thinking.

Your intuition can also enable you to be at your best during the *10 Seconds to Wealth*. Your intuition can guide you to say the right things to close a sale or enhance a business relationship.

Take action with your new ideas and you may allow an inflow of financial abundance. (Now, wouldn't that be great?)

How Healthy Humility Protects Your Energy

First, holding a rigid stance takes a lot of energy. Stop wasting your energy! Second, when you have access to your intuition, things start to flow the way you prefer. That's right. You can avoid struggle and the wasted energy associated with it!

With healthy humility, you have access to your intuition, which brings amazing opportunities and even joy.

How? Healthy humility gives you flexibility. In essence, flexibility means you can learn from life, your mentors, and even from your friends. You realize that human beings have a limited perception in the moment. It's like a friend warning you about the spinach on your teeth. Before the alert from your friend, you were oblivious to the spinach problem. You say "Thanks," and then remove the spinach.

Mistake: Thinking that humility is to feel less than others.
Solution: Deem healthy humility as an undemanding and flexible approach to learning and being in the moment.

Stand shoulder-to-shoulder with others. Recognize that each of us has limited perceptions in the moment.

We get into trouble when we make judgments about how people should act. Should people say "please" and "thank you"? Imagine you step back from a demanding stance and instead focus on your preferences. We all prefer when people are courteous and say "thank you." With healthy humility, you merely step back and just let people be as they are. (Note that there are times when people must step away from abuse and get professional help.)

Healthy humility is also a gift because, in a way, it lets you off the hook. We can't control other people's behavior and feelings. I remind myself with this phrase: "I don't run that show."

Healthy humility helps us live in the moment and feel better. How? We learn to add helpful thoughts:
- I don't run that show.
- I enter each moment fresh.
- I prefer to . . .
- I wonder . . .
- I wonder what I'm going to learn here.

Here's the secret: The ideas discussed here allow you to be flexible and avoid wallowing in upset feelings for most of the day. People who are flexible are fun to be around, which means that others easily and naturally bring them opportunities.

One of my book editors said, "Wait a minute. Are you asking people to pretend there are no problems?" My reply: "No! I'm suggesting that we become strategic about how we use our limited time and energy." The example I gave her concerned a couple that chose to devote their energy to feeling good when they were together during the week. For some disagreements they chose to say, "We'll save that for our couple's therapy session on Wednesday." This strategy allowed them to enjoy better times throughout the rest of the week.

Try healthy humility. It takes humility to let go and just observe whether you're welcoming intuition or getting tangled in fear.

Fear or Intuition—How can you tell?

Ever been confronted with a tough decision that was torturing you?

Have you thought: Should I do this or that? Will I get hurt? Will I deeply regret not attempting this action?

I hear you.

Many years ago I was confronted with the choice of taking a particular job. I chose to use the Benjamin Franklin Method. I pulled out a sheet of paper and wrote "Pro" on the left side and "Con" on the right side. I divided the sheet by drawing a vertical line down the center.

I quickly wrote nine positive reasons to take the job: good money, good location, and more. After that I wrote down the first two reasons against taking the job. Then, the third reason practically leapt off the page at me.

Boom! My intuition yelled: *Don't take the job.*

Logic would have said: You have more reasons to take the job than to not take the job.

But the one powerful reason against it turned my thoughts. Without my intuition, I probably would have taken the job, and I would have endured a painful experience.

My sweetheart said, "It's like your one reason against taking the job was a watermelon, and the nine reasons for the job were peas."

I make space for my intuition whenever possible. If I don't need to make a quick decision, I put in what I call "think-space." I'll say something like: "That sounds like a promising idea. I'll need to talk with my team about it. How about I get back to you tomorrow afternoon?"

My clients ask this big question: What's the difference between the voice of fear and the voice of intuition?

Over the years I've talked this over with psychologists, counselors, authors, and spiritually minded people. I learned that the difference is:

- *Fearful voice says:* contract, protect yourself, hide
- *Intuitive voice says:* expand, try something, explore, learn, grow, experiment

Certainly, when you're deciding whether taking a particular action is an appropriate risk to take, it is helpful to have a system. A good system would include a process to observe the whole situation and reduce the chances of bad outcomes. Also, the system would give you time (preferably with writing in a personal journal) to think through the situation and connect with your feelings.*

[* Discussions on systems to choose appropriate risk are included in my book *Soar! Nothing Can Stop You This Year: How to Unleash Your Hidden Power to Persuade Well, Get More Done, Gain Sudden Profits, Command Intuition and Feel Great*. View a free chapter at Amazon.com]

And it is still helpful to ask yourself:

- What is the voice really saying? Is it saying "fear" or "love"?
- Is this a chance for personal growth and possibility?
- Is the voice connected to fear? Is it connected to success or failure?

So many of my favorite activities in life involve stepping forward even when fear might try to hold me back (writing books, giving speeches, acting in films and more).

There is always the first time. Imagine this: to transform to a butterfly, a caterpillar must let go of fear.

So, make space for your intuition.

We can find our true path when we connect to our true self that is deeper and beyond fear. Your true self is that part of you that is naturally courageous, brilliant and connected with the good in the universe. You'll need to pull back from the surface noise of fear. Using healthy humility will help you access your intuition.

Principle: Live with healthy humility and welcome your intuition.

Power Questions: How can you devote some time and space before you make a decision. How can you welcome your intuition?

* * * * * *

Voice (Forgiveness)

"I'm cancelling Father's Day," Mia's father said. Then he went on to shun her for two months. Her father refused to come to the phone when she called. He would leave the house when Mia visited her mother.

This was breaking Mia down. She was my client and her tears broke my heart.

"He won't forgive me," she said. I asked her what had happened. She said her father hadn't heard her say "thank you" for the birthday gift he had given her, although she was sure she had said it. But the truth was that this was nothing new. I once asked her to draw a picture of what her father was like, and she drew a volcano. Her father would blow up and shun her for months every year, which was a cause of great anger for Mia.

Now, I ask you. Is there someone who has hurt you? Someone you might need to forgive? Or, do you feel that person doesn't deserve forgiveness?

I hear you.

But the truth is: Forgiveness is about freeing *you* from pain.

Forgiveness is a gift to you. It gives you more time to feel good and whole.

How?

I once appeared alongside Dr. Fred Luskin as a guest on a TV show. He said something I will always remember: "Forgiveness is about ending the cycle of blame and suffering. Forgiveness is when you become the hero of your own story."

Profound ideas.

If Mia feels her father is ruining her life, then she is not the hero of her own story. Also, let's face it, her father appears to be self-righteous and seems unlikely to change. So, Mia has choices. Hard choices. Here's what she does:

- When Mia feels angry when her father shuns her, she lets the thoughts come and go. That is, she lets them flow away like leaves on a river.
- Mia reminds herself that her father is unskilled at dealing with his own upset feelings.
- Mia reminds herself that her father has driven away all his friends, and his behavior is no different with her.
- Mia decides to continue visiting her mother, but she decides to visit for only one hour at a time. In this way, Mia limits her exposure to her father's negativity.

Note that none of this is about Mia waiting for her father to change.

How is her behavior forgiving? Specifically, when Mia reminds herself that her father is unskilled at dealing with his own upset feelings, she chooses to avoid sending him angry letters that attempt to straighten him out. She avoids returning negativity for negativity. She avoids trying to fix him.

Within the word "forgiveness" are the letters that spell the word "free."

I ask Mia, "When you have angry feelings about your father, do you sometimes run a vengeful fantasy in your mind?"

"Yes, how did you know?" she asked.

"I have people to forgive. And sometimes I need to forgive myself, too," I replied.

I continued, "The idea is for you to be the hero. Nurture yourself. Take yourself out of abusive situations. Get professional help if you need to. And don't let your father take up too much of your precious mental time."

"But how am I practicing forgiveness?" Mia asked.

"Have you decided to never visit your parents?" I asked.

"No," she replied.

"Then you're allowing your parents to be who they are. Don't forget they're from a different generation. They handle things the way they know how to handle them."

I continued, "This is important. You can forgive someone and not allow them to abuse you. And you can choose to avoid being vengeful toward a mean person."

It took time, but Mia filled her life with being around friendly people. Her pain quieted down. She now makes sure to get plenty of sleep before visiting her parents so that she has ample energy to be patient and helpful.

I shared with her an important part of forgiveness: the difference between judgment and discernment.

Judgment implies taking a superior attitude toward someone—like a judge sitting on the bench high above a lowly defendant.

On the other hand, discernment implies "recognizing." With discernment, you recognize that the other person is doing the best he can, although his hurtful behavior is inappropriate. When necessary, limit your exposure to that person for a time period.

When we decide to let our thoughts flow from condemnation to compassion, we often discover that we ultimately feel lighter and even freer.

This is the tip of the iceberg. The process of forgiveness is a lengthier discussion. I invite you to learn more. It's truly worth the effort.

How to "Do" Forgiveness

So many speakers mention the value of forgiveness. I wondered: What is a tangible action I can do to begin the forgiveness process?

Here is the action: Focus on *Just One More Thought*. This is your step to success, peace and connection.

What's your first thought when you see someone you don't like?
- "Ugh, he's here. What mean thing is he going to say today?"
- "Oh, I wish she would just go away!"

How about with family members?
- "She doesn't care about my feelings."
- "What an angry person. He's so critical."

Here's a simple step that can bring more success, peace and connection to your life:

Let the first thought float by and let in a new thought.

Let's look at the above thought: "What an angry person. He's so critical."

What would an alternative thought sound like? How about: "What a frightened person. He doesn't know how to interact well with others."

Some people would take this second thought (frightened

person) and feel some compassion for that person.

Use compassion as your compass.

The idea here is that many of us have been conditioned to react to stimuli with judgmental thoughts.

With practice, our next thought can be a "discernment thought."

Here's the difference:
- A *judgmental thought* puts you at a distance. It puts you metaphorically on a high-up bench looking down on the person, like you are superior and judging them.
- A *discernment thought* helps you *recognize* that the person is trying to cope the best she or he can.

The transition from judgment to discernment helps you calm down. It helps you become stronger so that you make a positive response. So, how do we make that transition?

We take a breath. We are quiet. We let another thought arise.

When you're stuck in a judgmental thought, ask yourself: "How can I view this with compassion? How can I connect with this person?"

These are powerful questions. They come from a place of compassion in yourself—that is, from your true self. The ego self (often called the false self) is the fragile part of you that feels small and vulnerable.

When I talk about "voice" and "forgiveness," I'm suggesting that we listen to the compassionate voice in ourselves. That's the voice of our true self, which is naturally courageous, brilliant and loving.

Remember, judgment is *not* connection. Judgment creates space and separation from other people.

So remember: Let that first thought flow by as if it were on a river. Take a breath and know that another thought will come next.

You'll be glad to enjoy more harmony.

Principle: Let a judgment thought flow by and welcome a discernment thought.

Power Questions: How can you recognize a judgment thought? How can you nurture yourself so you can welcome forgiving thoughts?

* * * * * *

Inspire (faith)

What's the secret to more success and happiness?

To understand this, you need to have an experience. This doesn't mean just an intellectual understanding of the experience.

What experience are we talking about? An experience of faith. Whoa! Stop! We're not going to talk about faith in the usual way. Let's try something else. Try substituting the word "faith" with "empowering stance."

Why? Because that's what faith gives you. The empowering stance is your springboard to a positive approach from moment-to-moment. And, we notice that faith is important to various spiritual paths.

Have you given up on something? Have too many disappointments gotten you to back off from life? Have you stopped going for your heartfelt dreams? Do you believe only lucky people get to experience the joy of a dream fulfilled?

I hear you. It appears that many of us have allowed our faith to be squelched by doubt. Where does that doubt come from? Disappointment. Pain. Sadness.

I am with you on this. I carry my own painful experiences. And I carry faith, too. A faith that I have nurtured to be bigger than disappointment, pain and sadness.

How?

It's a choice I make moment to moment.

I choose to act from a base of:
- I can learn from everything I experience.
- Higher Power is supporting me.

These two points help my courage, compassion and empathy to grow.

Use compassion as your compass.

Have you noticed that "compass" and "compassion" are different by only three letters?

Faith can serve you as a compass and as an energy source. When you have faith, you try more things and you take appropriate risks.

Why? Because it is worth it!

I have talked with people from various spiritual paths, and I have discovered that they share a few viewpoints in common:
- Everything is for a purpose.
- Higher Power is looking out for me.
- I am not alone. I am supported.

Imagine that you felt these ideas deep in your heart. When you do, you start from a base of faith. And guess what? You likely feel better and stronger.

How do you get this faith or empowering stance?

You decide. Now. This moment. You make a choice. You say, "I want to experience more happy moments. I choose to live each moment with faith."

Even the atheists I know have faith in something. Often it's science and the betterment of human living through the application of reason.

You operate with faith every time you make a left turn in a busy intersection. Really? Yes. You have faith that your car won't stall at just that moment.

Each day we work with a certain level of faith—our empowering stance.

Now consider taking your faith to a higher level.

What's at stake? Your willingness to put more energy to expanding the horizons of your life. I have a friend who places comfort above everything else. He has a college degree that he doesn't use at all. He works in a field unrelated to his true interests. Why? He doesn't have faith that he can—on any level—use his innate gifts and talents. I feel sad when I think about this.

But this is *not* for you.

Try something different. Get coaching. Study books relevant to your goal. Show the world that you can do something. Begin on a small scale. Step forward in faith.

Take the first step in faith. You don't have to see the whole staircase, just take the first step. – Martin Luther King, Jr.

Take your next step. I'll be cheering for you.

Principle: Choose to approach life with faith (the empowering stance).

Power Question: How can you embrace faith and reassure yourself that you are supported by the people around you and by Higher Power?

* * * * * *

Nurture (grace)

Have you ever felt overwhelmed? Have you ever been out of personal energy?

How about discouraged and sad?

Take a breath. We're going to cover some solutions that can help you feel peace and comfort in the moment.

I once felt slammed down by life. I sought help from an older friend. In an almost a flippant way, he said, "In life, you do your duty."

During that time, which was emotional and when I hit bottom, I realized that a moral and ethical life calls for self-discipline. But then I realized something else. It took a lot for me to admit this to myself: I do my duty and it's not making me happy.

So, I ask you, what else is there?

Grace. Ever see someone who is graceful? Figure skater Kristi Yamaguchi jumps to my mind. Certainly, she demonstrates great athleticism. But one detail that stands out is the sheer grace in her hand movements. Her efforts plus her talent create her grace. Her grace is a gift—to her and to us.

Physical grace is easy to see. And, many of us have witnessed someone act with grace. It can be as simple as the time I saw a salesperson bring calm to a situation with an angry customer. She said, "Yes. You're right this is a frustrating situation. And I'm listening carefully to you. I will help you with this."

How can you experience grace?

Three words: *Shift to gratitude.*

Many people express that their experience of grace is like a gift from Higher Power. We'll talk about that soon.

Meanwhile, let me share a practical, everyday example of *shifting to gratitude.* Several years ago I visited Disneyland with a friend. I felt terrific to be in a place that celebrates courtesy and creativity. Unfortunately, my friend felt terrible because she didn't have the money to purchase all the souvenirs she wanted.

Although I had less money in my pocket than she did, my thoughts were immersed in joy and gratitude. Just to be at Disneyland was a gift.

What can you do when there is no immediate physical solution?

Make a shift in your perception. Shift to gratitude.

Three Steps towards Grace: Awareness, Openness & Experience

When is grace needed? When someone close to you says something that feels like a denial of your right to have or experience your own feelings.

Some time ago, a relative said to me: "You have no reason to be upset." This was simply not true in light of the particular situation and the injuries I had endured in the past from that person.

But here's the big shift: I seek to learn from every moment. So I did a "turnaround" with the words: "You have no reason to be upset."

Turnaround: "I have every reason to nurture myself and be around nurturing influences."

Clearly, this relative was someone to step away from for a period of time.

Let's apply the Three Steps of Grace.

Awareness: What are the positive elements of my life? What gifts do I have?

Openness: Will I let the positive elements in my life inspire positive feelings?

Experience: Will I give myself 10 seconds to experience this positivity?

As we covered earlier, recent brain research notes that it takes 10 seconds of focus for a positive experience to impact our long-term memory. This is one of the reasons that writing in a journal every night (and logging good things that happened that day) helps you physically change your brain cells. This is related to what science calls brain plasticity. *If you write in your journal each night, you will literally experience your life as good—and full of grace.*

You've been given grace, but may not feel it in the moment.

My Disneyland example is just a small demonstration of the idea of shifting to gratitude. You need to become *aware* of the gifts in your life in this present moment. Then you can shift to be *open* to something positive, and you *experience* the gift of that positive part of your life.

How You Can Experience "Grace Under Pressure"

Imagine you can turn around distress and actually enter an empowered state of being. This happens when you prepare and rehearse. The idea is to rehearse positive patterns so that they become your new and improved default setting when something goes wrong.

When people are under stress they fall back to the patterns and behaviors in their established default settings. Many of us take a distressing thought and, metaphorically, hold it so close to our eyes that we cannot see anything else. At that moment we cannot feel the grace that is actually present in our lives.

Imagine if someone offers you $20,000 to recite 10 good things in your life at this present moment. You could do it. You'd find the gifts in your life—the grace.

My quick list would include:
- I love my sweetheart and she loves me.
- I'm grateful to be sharing helpful methods with you through this book, which I'm hopeful will bring you and your loved ones more peace, comfort and fulfillment.
- I'm grateful for my excellent health.
- I'm grateful for my family, friends, students, readers, clients, audiences and so much more.

To experience *grace under pressure*, you need to train

yourself to shift the direction of your thinking. For example, I sometimes get *tired* grading the work of my graduate students. When fatigue overcomes me, I tap my fist on my thigh as I tell myself, "I can do this!" I have trained myself to respond to this self-designed trigger. My energy revs up and I complete the work.

Here is a trigger you can use to shift the direction of your thoughts: Say, "I am grateful for …" Then express the gifts and the blessings that are in your life.

Other Sources for Feeling Grace in the Moment

As an instructor of college-level Comparative Religion, I note that many spiritual paths emphasize grace as "unmerited favor" from Higher Power. Many people believe that Higher Power gives us inner peace, inner strength and even guidance. They believe that we cannot earn something so grand as Higher Power's favor.

Those who seek to have a fulfilling connection and relationship with Higher Power often engage in practices such as meditation, prayer, spiritual retreats and more. These activities can provide a sense that there is a reason for what they endure, and that benevolent Higher Power is providing opportunities for *growing in courage, compassion and their ability to express love.*

Here is a trigger you can use to shift the direction of your thoughts. My clients say phrases like:
- Thank you Higher Power for the blessings I have.
- Thank you God for my job and for the steady work.
- Thank you Universe for all the good in my life.

Pick what works for you. The point is to acknowledge and then feel the grace given to you from Higher Power.

I invite you to explore a number of practices such as

meditation, prayer and spiritual retreats so that you learn to experience grace in the present moment. Grace is a gift you already have. You'll need to look beyond the concerns that the ego obsesses over in order to find the grace within you. The ego, or the false self, is that part of you that feels small and vulnerable.

On the other hand, your true self is that part of you that is naturally courageous and brilliant and feels connected with all that is good. Your true self feels the grace that you have already been given.

You are so weak. Give up to grace. The ocean takes care of each wave till it gets to shore. – Rumi

What do you give up? The obsessions of the ego. Turn your focus to the gifts in your life. On a visible and practical level, find good feelings by *appreciating what you already have*. Also, find the good feeling by *enjoying the journey* as you take action toward your goals.

How grace can help open floodgates of financial abundance

Use grace as part of your business dealings, including for persuasion, sales, deal making and negotiations. How? Use the methods in this book to condition yourself to be at your best during the crucial 10 seconds that will make a difference. The truth is, gaining wealth is often based on your ability to enhance a relationship, which can happen in 10 seconds. In 10 seconds you can win the sale or lose the deal. In 10 seconds you can create agreement or you can create disharmony.

For grace in the moment, you need to start with two things
- Pure intention
- Natural confidence

When I train graduate students in the art and science of persuasion, I emphasize:

Pure intention keeps in mind the benefit to the listener.

That is, your good intention is to do something helpful for the person with whom you're talking.

The opposite is manipulation: pulling strings without concern for the other person's well being.

Now we turn to the second part of grace in the moment: natural confidence.

Natural confidence is expressing your natural brilliance.

The opposite is being phony and being a mediocre copy of someone else.

Pure intention and natural confidence come together to make you *graceful* during those crucial 10 seconds. And when you're graceful, you turn an average 10 seconds into *10 Seconds to Wealth*.

To access your natural confidence, remember to:
- Keep in mind the benefit to the listener.
- Discover what you do well. (Perhaps, you're a good listener.)
- Express your natural brilliance.

As we discussed, many people feel that grace is a gift from Higher Power. Accept the gift while expressing your gratitude. My clients often say, "I'm grateful for steady work."

Want to feel grace in the moment? Say aloud: "I am grateful for …"

Want to take the experience of grace to another level? Say aloud: "Thank you [Higher Power] for . . ."

Principle: Express your natural brilliance, accept the gift of grace, and experience natural confidence.

Power Question: How can you nurture and express what you are good at?

Express (Art)

Ever watch a movie that moved you to tears? That movie is a form of art.

Years ago, I rode as a passenger in a car driven by a friend. The car was *pummeled* by another vehicle! A car accident. My friend Gene stayed with me for hours at the emergency room. He remained with me while I was stretched out in a neck brace and got scanned and x-rayed. He was there when I confronted the tough question: "How bad is this and what's next?"

Gene was expressing another form of art: the art of friendship and support.

What does art do? It creates. Often it creates feelings.

Unfortunately, many of us forget that every human being is truly an artist—that is, a creator. The mere fact that you are reading these words means you have adapted to all that life has thrown your way so far. Good for you! And it's likely you have needed to be creative on a number of occasions.

Author Seth Godin wrote, "Art is made by a human being. Art is created to have an impact, to change someone else. Art is a gift. You can sell the souvenir, the canvas, the recording . . . but the idea itself is free, and the generosity is a critical part of making art. By my definition, most art has nothing to do with oil paint or marble. Art is what we're doing when we do our best work."

In the book *The Gift: Creativity and the Artist in the Modern World*, author Lewis Hyde writes that, although we may buy a ticket to a theatrical performance, the play is actually a gift that we receive from the artists involved in the production. One of my editors said: "That is so true. I went to a concert of chamber music for the first time. It was such a gift. One piece consumed me and I felt such emotion that I began to cry. It was the first time in my life I ever cried while experiencing the art of music. The piece was by Franz Shubert. I later purchased the CD."

My point here is that you can experience a source of happiness when you *own* your art, that is, when you express yourself. I'm told that there is even an art to making coffee. (That's not my drink. But I know about making a cookies and cream milkshake!)

There's an art to writing a letter to a friend or romantic partner. For example, one of my best moments in life was when I got the idea to write a letter to my sweetheart. It was brief. I wrote: "Thank you for S-t-r-e-t-c-h-i-n-g." (I made the word span 21 inches, two sheets of paper). I was acknowledging how she demonstrates flexibility in regards to my full schedule. She loved the letter and it continues to hang on our bathroom mirror. You see: Art gets appreciated.

I invite you now to look around. Where is life calling you to express yourself? What can you do in an artful (creative, perhaps life-enhancing) way?

Art gives twice: to the receiver and to the person expressing herself.

You have Divine Gifts just by being a person. You were designed (part of your standard equipment) to be creative and to be able to create art. Do not get caught up in the traditional meaning of art or what it means to be an artist. Art is not just a movie, painting or craftwork. I have friends who created a wonderful family life with a loving, supportive home atmosphere. That's important. And that's art, too.

It takes some effort. But when you devote that extra effort, you find that you're really living!

Start today. Start this hour. Find a way to express yourself. Be an artist!

This world needs each of us to give the gift of our natural brilliance. Thank you for contributing.

Now is the time. Only you can express the art that you are on this planet to express.

Principle: Each person can express art because each person has the standard equipment that makes up of his or her Divine Gifts: love, humility, forgiveness, grace and art.

Power Question: How can you express yourself in a giving, artful way?

* * * * * *

Conclusion to
January – New Beginnings Chapter
(Divine Gifts)

We have explored the six Divine Gifts in each of us:

1. Decide (love)
2. Intuit (humility)
3. Voice (forgiveness)
4. Inspire (faith)
5. Nurture (grace)
6. Express (art)

The Divine Gifts are your standard equipment. As you learn to express them, you are also conditioning yourself to be at your best during the *10 Seconds to Wealth*. You'll notice that your Divine Gifts help you stay in a positive state of being.

When you express your Divine Gifts you are naturally confident, courageous, charismatic and attractive. You draw in positive people who bring opportunities. Those who express their natural confidence and goodwill are the people who receive many offers and opportunities.

I see this frequently with my clients. When they enter the empowered state of being, and when they express their

Divine Gifts, they light up any room they are in. People are attracted to those who shine their natural light. They are the ones who are alive and ready for the next challenge.

I don't believe people are looking for the meaning of life as much as they are looking for the experience of being alive.

– Joseph Campbell

People who express their Divine Gifts feel fully alive. The energy flows from them in positive waves. People nearby want to have some of that radiance to rub off on them.

Here's a practical example:

I once gave a free presentation to help job-seekers do well in job interviews. One attendee came up and said, "You should speak for ACME Company."

During the speech I expressed my Divine Gifts, and it felt good. I responded to his kind suggestion with *four sentences that brought in $329,067.*

Are you ready for the sentences?

I replied: "Thank you. Who should I talk with? Do you have her number? How about we leave a message for her now."

At that moment the attendee called the person I needed to talk to and left an enthusiastic message on my behalf. Soon I had a meeting with the person. My total income for the presentations I made for the company brought in $329,067.

Do you see how expressing our Divine Gifts brings in new opportunities?

Quickly Access Your Divine Gifts

What do you want? For some of us, that may take a few moments to express. Here's an approach you can try. Answer these questions:
- What's going on in my life that I do *not* want?
- What is it that I would like to change?

To quickly access your Divine Gifts, it helps to ask empowering questions.
- What gifts are in my life right now? (grace)
- How can I connect with "I am love"? (love)
- What am I learning now? (humility)
- How can I express my creativity and kindness? (art)
- How am I being supported now? (faith)
- How can I see the big picture and look on it with compassion? (forgiveness)
- How can I get coaching? (humility)
- How is Higher Power helping me? (grace)

To be at your best in those all-important 10 seconds, which will help you do well in business, consider these questions:
- How can I turn this problem into a chance to enhance my relationship with the customer? (humility)
- How can I express appreciation for my co-worker? (art)
- How can I make this person feel important? (love)
- How can we, as a team, make this situation better? (faith)
- How can I let go of my frustration and support my team members to get back on track? (forgiveness)
- How can I flow with this situation and make the best of it? (grace)

Here's another way to quickly access your Divine Gifts: Focus on *Just One More Thought*.

For many of us, our default setting is to make a judgment for whatever arises. But to be at your best in the *10 Seconds to*

Wealth, let that judgment-thought flow by as if it's a leaf on a river. Welcome the next thought. If you're stuck in judgment, ask this question: "How can I look at this with compassion?"

Access Divine Gifts with a Simple Shift in Thought

Imagine that you keep a log of the thoughts you have throughout your day. How many of them would be some variation of "I *have* to do this"? It's likely that you complain a lot to yourself.

Instead, to access your Divine Gifts, simply shift your thought to "I *get* to do this."

For example, a main component of my graduate school teaching responsibilities is to grade student papers. Most teachers complain about this chore. Instead of saying to myself, "I *have* to grade papers," I tell myself: "I *get to* grade papers." How? *I get the chance to encourage each student.* That simple change in language helps me to get excited about the chore. It makes me feel truly connected to my purpose.

My mission: *I help people experience enthusiasm, love and wisdom to fulfill big dreams.*

So, I *get to* encourage my students.

I invite you to transform "I have to" into "I get to." Then ask yourself "How?"

This is your step to accessing your Divine Gifts. Look for the opportunity.

The Secret to Quickly Access Your Divine Gifts

The coaching staff on a successful football team memorizes the plays. There is no time to look down at a stack of paper when the game is being played.

Using this strategy, I invite you to memorize the methods and words that touch your heart as you read this book. This

will help you become ready for the *10 Seconds to Wealth*. For example, you could memorize:
- Replace "I have to" with "I get to."
- Remember your Divine Gifts: love, humility, forgiveness, grace, faith and art.
- Think: How can I look at this with compassion?

Pick any method in this book that captures your attention.

Remember: *People under stress tend to fall back to negative default settings.*

But this is *not* for you. Your life is *more* important than a football game.

Memorize methods and rehearse using them. Condition yourself to be better today than yesterday. Over and over, my clients say: "Tom, I memorized that method and I had it in mind when I was in the stressful situation. It made all the difference."

Memorize the methods and tools in this book and you can easily access your Divine Gifts.

Expressing your Divine Gifts helps you create a wealth of financial abundance, better friendships, more love and even inner peace.

The rest of this book covers specific topics that help you to condition yourself to express your Divine Gifts.

Here is a principle for your *Year of Awesome:*
Principle #1: Share in your Divine Gifts.

Power Question: How will you make space in your daily life to notice and express your Divine Gifts?

February – Valentine's Day and Approach the Moment with Love

Valentine's Day, for years, filled me with fear. Why? As a young man, trying to be a good boyfriend, I looked on Valentine's Day as a minefield. So many ways things could go wrong!

I finally figured out a way to do well. I asked my sweetheart, *"What would give you a good Valentine's Day?"*

She told me the *Fabulous Five* (my term):
1. Balloon
2. Chocolate
3. Dinner
4. Card
5. Flowers

If I provide the Fabulous Five, I cannot go wrong.

I've heard some people complain that Valentine's Day is a made-up holiday to make greeting card companies and flower-vendors money.

I learned to use what I call a *SwitchPhrase*. I tell myself: *"This is an opportunity for me to be loving and show my appreciation for my sweetheart."*

Think of how relationships go sour. Is it because a partner received too much appreciation and kindness? No!

Here's our next principle for your *Year of Awesome:*
Principle #2: Uplift through "the most important"

I emphasize "uplift" because in my early, faulty approach

to Valentine's Day I was down in the mud of fear of making a mistake. As I mentioned, I turned things around by asking my sweetheart, "What would give you a good Valentine's Day?"

Another version of this question is: **"What's most important to you about _____?"**

When I learn what is most important to a person and I *take action* related to that, I can do well!

We can use the A.C.T. process:

A - appreciate

C – care (compassion)

T – trade away judgment (welcome discernment)

1. Appreciate

So I learned to focus on Valentine's Day as an opportunity to show appreciation for my sweetheart.

Who in your life needs your appreciation? Another viewpoint is: With whom would you like more harmony?

Take appropriate action.

2. Care (compassion)

"If you want other people to be happy, practice compassion. If you want to be happy, practice compassion." – The Dalai Lama

Compassion is defined as "a feeling of deep sympathy and sorrow for another who is stricken by misfortune, accompanied by a strong desire to alleviate the suffering." (dictionary.com)

"People don't care how much you know until they know how much you care." – John C. Maxwell

What is one of the most powerful ways to show that you care? Ask a question, demonstrate your interest and *listen.*

One time an elderly relative was ranting and telling me how wrong he thought I was. I replied, "You're not listening. Don't you want to listen?"

"No."

At that point, I realized that this person really did not care about my feelings and my experience.

I disengaged from the conversation as soon as possible.

Listening is hard work. As an Executive Coach, I do a lot of listening. This means that I also need to do a lot of recharging so I can be fully compassionate and intuitive in the moment—during a coaching session with my client.

Asking "What is most important to you about ___?" is a good start to the process.

3. Trade away judgment (welcome discernment)

In significant ways, an opposite approach to compassion is being judgmental. When we're judgmental we function like a judge, pronouncing other people to be "guilty." We even pass down sentences (in our mind).

People can feel another person's judgmental thoughts and feelings. We can see such judgment and rigidity on their face and hear it in the person's tone of voice.

There IS a solution ...

Substitute Discernment for being Judgmental

Discernment is flexible. You observe and you can allow new data in. Judgment is about the past and being rigid. Discernment is about being in this present moment. You can assess the situation, *and* have room to change your perception and to change your mind in light of new information.

"*Discernment is flowing like water.*" – *Moonwater SilverClaw*

* * *

A number of people report that they are "spiritual." What does it take to be spiritual? Part of the process is to be fully present in this current moment. We also make efforts to listen and express our compassion.

When you engage in the A.C.T. process, you truly approach this moment with love.

Here is a principle for your *Year of Awesome*:
Principle #2: Uplift through "the most important"

Power Question: How will you ask questions to find out what is most important to the other person? (Consider asking: "What's most important to you about ____?")

March – March 4th ("March Forth")

My client Harry told me that he always remembers the idea of "march forth."

During our conversation, I asked, "Would you like a simple 2-minute method to help you sleep better and get more done during the next day?"

"Yes!"

I introduced my *Top Six Targets* (top priorities) that I write on a 3x5 card just before I go to sleep. This clears my mind, fostering better sleep. When I wake up, I already have my "marching orders."

This relates to …

Principle #3: Concentrate on *Top Six Targets*

When you note your Top Six Targets and take action to accomplish them, you'll feel better! Each day becomes more productive. You see your progress clearly.

With audiences, I emphasize: "Two for you, two for family, two for work."

The *Top Six Targets* process functions as a vital tool to improve your productivity *and* your morale.

We'll explore two other vital elements (described below): your *9-Minute Miracle Breakthrough* and your *Momentum Action Plan (MAP)*.

Make Money Through Your Natural Brilliance

In the previous section "Divine Gifts," you learned how to

develop the mindset to expand your prosperity. So now the important thing is to progress forward. This section covers the 9-Minute Miracle Breakthrough. Once you learn the process, you can devote just nine minutes a day or even once a week to identifying what will really move you toward your dreams.

With the 9-Minute Miracle Breakthrough, I help my clients bring the process of prosperity expansion down to daily, individually tailored steps.

In this section, we will learn how to earn more money. Let's remember that money is a tool. For now, this affirmation is helpful: *Money is a tool that I use well for the benefit of all.* When you really feel this positive energy, you wake up your spirit to prosperity. We can see this process at work with Oprah Winfrey. Millions of people find her to be genuine and generous. And Oprah is the first African-American woman billionaire in U.S. history.

In this section you will create a Momentum Action Plan™ (MAP) as part of the 9-Minute Miracle Breakthrough. When you implement the Momentum Action Plan on a daily basis, you enjoy a new zest in your moment-to-moment experiences. You will also learn to use leverage, which means gaining the most benefit from the least effort.

My clients have found the 9-Minute Miracle Breakthrough to be more beneficial than standard time management and goal-setting practices. You will learn to use the power that is already inside you.

Science of the 9-Minute Miracle Breakthrough process

Over the years I developed the Science of Emotional Leverage™. The best way to describe leverage is with an image:

Imagine that you want to move a boulder. You place a

small rock on the ground near the boulder. The small rock is your fulcrum. Then you use a big stick as your lever to move the boulder. With little effort you get big results. That's leverage.

Emotional Leverage is a strategy that utilizes your emotions to help you get big results with little effort. Emotional Leverage is how you free yourself for success.

Many people get frustrated and give up when they begin new methods or strategies—only to fall back to old habits. This disappointing situation results from a structural error in traditional training. When returning to old habits, these people are just waving around the proverbial stick and not using the key device, which is the fulcrum (or a little rock in our leverage metaphor).

The fulcrum represents merging with your True Self. Your True Self is the part of you that is naturally brilliant and courageous. On the other hand, the False Self (also known as the Ego) is the part of you that is stuck in fear and feels caged. That's why we want to focus on your True Self—to help you free yourself from fear.

Make your True Self a bigger part of your daily life

Merging with your True Self is the process by which you consciously direct your thoughts away from fear and toward the perspective of abundance and spiritual growth. Eventually, like learning to ride a bicycle, you can maintain balance without conscious effort. The more you practice viewing life from your True Self, the more you experience merging with your True Self. Many people express that regular sessions of prayer or meditation help them experience inner peace. Such inner peace is a manifestation of the True Self.

This experience of inner peace is what martial arts

masters refer to as being centered. Similarly, when Olympic athletes are "in the zone," they are focused. Creative people like writers talk about how words flow effortlessly. The point is that our emotions serve us to be productive when we merge with our True Self.

Your True Self saves you from procrastination.

Fear leads many of us to procrastinate. We seek to avoid pain. The good news is that the ten steps of the 9-Minute Miracle Breakthrough shift our attention away from pain. We get a new focus point. We do not shut down because of pain. Instead, we begin with four questions to connect with the True Self.

At this point, pull out sheet of paper, notepad or a journal to write down questions and answers. By participating in the following process, you will form a roadmap to your best life. This roadmap is your Momentum Action Plan (MAP).

To be clear: When you go through the 9-Minute Miracle Breakthrough process, you end up with your Momentum Action Plan.

In the Momentum Action Plan, you will be answering ten questions.

Momentum Action Plan (MAP)

Question 1: What do you want?

Choose any area in which you desire something. In just twenty seconds, write down whatever comes to mind. It can be a thing, a relationship, a new job, financial freedom, anything.

My clients have written:
- I want a new car.
- I want some new business clothes.
- I want my husband to treat me better.
- I want a career that satisfies my need for more prosperity, enriching friendships and exotic travel.

- I want to get a particular project done.

So write down what you want. Just a few words can be powerful.

This reminds me of a time when my parents and I were vacationing at Universal Studios. It was the first time I could show my parents part of my world as a motion picture director. It was also the first time that I pushed my mother in a wheelchair. Her walking had become limited as the result of a long illness. I felt my heart cringe each time I helped my mother transfer from the wheelchair to a chair on an attraction. Her once strong arms trembled, and her face tensed when she stood on her weakened legs. It was a strange contrast to be with my family in a park built for pleasure, and to be so conscious of my mother's pain.

Actors strolled by portraying characters like Laurel and Hardy, Mae West and The Director, who wore riding pants and boots and held a megaphone. The Director took one look at my mother in the wheelchair and said, "No more stunts for you!"

My mother burst into laughter, and my father and I joined her. It was delightful to see my mother's response. What was real here? My mother's pain and infirmity were real, but in just a moment our perceptions changed, and we enjoyed laughter and connection. Our revised perceptions helped us notice more than pain and infirmity in that particular moment.

My point is this: *It took just five words to change how we felt.* When you write down what you want, remember that just a few words can be powerful. And it's part of connecting with your True Self.

You are connecting with your True Self when you emphasize the good, the blessed and the abundance in the moment. Using a few powerful words gives you a pivot point for your thoughts and feelings.

It's the process of *Align with Your Design.*

Consider that whatever you write down immediately may be just the tip of the iceberg. For example, I might say I want to finish writing a children's book. But there's something deeper to it than that—which leads us to the second question ...

Momentum Action Plan (MAP)
Question 2: No. Come on, what do you really want?

Often, beneath our initial thoughts about what we want, there is something even more crucial that we want even more.

For me, what's below the idea of creating a children's book is that I really want to make a contribution to brightening the lives of millions of people—something like the joy inspired by Walt Disney.

And what's even deeper is this: I really want to feel I have accomplished a great purpose and that I've lived a meaningful life.

My clients have said:
- I want a new job. But what I really want is an end to the stress and meaninglessness of my current job.
- I want a closer relationship. But what I really want is to feel safe to reveal my deep feelings to my romantic partner.

You'll notice that we're talking about feelings. And that leads us to the third question ...

Momentum Action Plan (MAP)
Question 3: Better yet, what do you want to feel?

It's important to focus on what you want to feel.

Remember the first four questions help you access your True Self. This third question gives us a special insight. What you want to feel is like an indicator light on a plane's control panel. This light reveals what your natural brilliance is.

In a previous section, I shared a quote from bestselling author Robert Allen: "When you're doing what you love to do, the money comes naturally. Maybe not at first, but eventually ... if you stick with it. Do you think Bob Hope started out with a goal, 'I want to become a millionaire by making people laugh, then I'll retire to do what I want'? I doubt it. He just did what he did best. And the money came."

We can imagine a moment or series of moments in which Bob Hope first made people laugh. He probably had the experience of "Oooh. I made them laugh. This feels good!"

Many of my clients have said, "I don't know what I want to do next with my life." The challenge then is to have them remember when they had an experience of "Oooh, this feels good!" We also need to remember moments of "Oooh, I'm good at this!"

Similarly, it may be time for my client to start trying new things to find out what brings the "Oooh!" feelings. How do you know if you will enjoy writing a song? You try it out.

How do you know if you will enjoy a cooking course? You attend a first class. By the way, I know a vivacious woman who has consistently tried new things and experienced success in different phases of her life. Let's look at her journey:

1. She began as a hair stylist.
2. She then owned her own salon. (15 years)
3. She sold the business and traveled the world.
4. She took an interest in graphic arts.
5. She earned a degree in graphic arts and worked as

an administrative assistant in a church, using her graphic arts skills. (5 years)
6. She completed a program with the California Culinary Academy and has prepared food for Pixar employees and for George Lucas (with Lucas' private chef).
7. She published her first children's book which appears in a number of languages.

It's important to know what you like; what feels good to you; what is fun for you. What feels great is often aligned with your natural brilliance. The idea is to align with your design. This means that you align with your gifts. Higher Power has given you natural brilliance and talents. It is up to you to experiment, to see how you feel, and then refine new skills.

Write down what you want to feel. Here's how this process goes:

Sarah (a client): How do I know what I want to feel?
Tom: Good question. I'll help with a few questions. What do you want?
Sarah: I want to publish a children's story.
Tom: That's great! And what do you really want?
Sarah: I want to make money using my talents.
Tom: And if you can make money by using your talents, how would you feel?
Sarah: I'd feel … I'd feel safe. I'd feel like I could always take care of myself.
Tom: Great. Write that down. You want to feel safe.

Connect with desired feelings with "See, Hear, Touch"

Often, when we hear a question, our mind gives us the answer in flashing images, or sounds or a feeling. At one point, I listened to Serena, one of my college students with a major in Motion Pictures and Television Production. She described what motivates her with making feature films: "I see the audience clapping; I hear the audience's laughter; and I feel a warm hug (touch) from my brother as he celebrates the accomplishment with me."

So write down what you want to feel and note your impressions of See, Hear and Touch.

Write quickly. Don't hesitate. It's just you and the paper. Remember your initial impressions are usually on target.

By the way, you can keep your answers confidential. *Often, when a dream is new and fragile, it helps to avoid revealing it.* Some people, even family members, can torpedo a dream.

When Walt Disney wanted to create Disneyland, no one understood it. There had never before been a clean, delightful theme park. Walt's wife and his brother Roy were both against the idea. The Board of Directors was against it. Walt had to cash in his life insurance to fund the initial research and design of Disneyland.

My point is that Walt Disney had an unusual faith in his own judgment, and many of us have not yet developed such a valuable faith. It may be best to keep quiet about our new dream until we have some tangible results in the right direction. For example, a friend of mine who is an associate editor of a magazine has recently completed a course in filmmaking. Two of the four films he made are quite effective. That's an important step forward.

The Momentum Action Plan that you're creating is for your eyes only (until you decide who is a real supporter of your dream). Now, let's continue ...

Momentum Action Plan (MAP)

Question 4: How can you experience the heart (core elements/the heart of the matter) on a small scale?

At a particular speech, I held up a prop—a heart-shaped box. What's inside your heart? What do you want to feel?

One of my clients told me she wants to be an Oscar-winning actress. I asked her, "Where is the joy for you in acting?"

"It's being in the moment. Feeling the presence of the audience. Feeling the thrill of being alive and expressing my energy when I'm on stage. I had that experience in a high school production," she replied.

Write down this vital question: *Where is the joy?*

Answering this question helps you break free from previous patterns of thinking.

The idea of Free Yourself for Success is to think in a different way. The goal is to develop an entirely different pattern of thinking.

What you want to find is the element that creates the joy. When you know what creates joy for you, you can start experiencing that joy this week—on a small scale.

This week my client can sign up for an acting class. This week my client can borrow a video camcorder and practice a monologue in front of it.

It's important to get to the heart of the matter.

This reminds me of a time, some years ago, when I was directing a feature film. My cast and crew were on the set, which was an airport runway. This was before the September 11th tragedies, which is why my crew could be on a tarmac without any complications.

The heart of the matter for me when I'm directing is to keep everyone safe—and make a good movie. A stuntman was preparing to jump from an airplane before it left the runway. Everyone was unaware that the wing was headed straight for the cameraman's head. The plane's engines would drown out any possible warning. The cameraman was standing too tall. I had a split second to make a decision because no one else could help. A director is like a ship's captain, responsible for everyone's safety. I made my decision. I ran to the cameraman, grabbed him by the jacket and pulled him down. The wing sliced the air where our heads had been! What I learned that day was to keep a constant vigil and then act on what my intuition tells me. And I learned to keep focusing on the Heart of the Matter.

The first four questions of the Momentum Action Plan help you to access your True Self. To see how these elements fit together, let's look at this example:

Momentum Action Plan (MAP) — Partial Example
What do you want?
To complete writing my children's book.
No. Come on, what do you really want?
To uplift the lives of millions of people in ways similar to what Walt Disney did.
Better yet, what do you want to feel?
To feel really alive. To feel the exuberance, a warm, full feeling in my chest (touch) when audience members laugh (hear) while watching an animated feature film I directed. To see big smiles as audience members rise from their seats at the end of the film.
How can you experience the heart (core elements/the heart of the matter) on a small scale?
The heart of the matter is to enjoy the excitement of collaboration—when people come together and make a "whole" that is better than the sum of its parts. I can enjoy the process of working with the artist, and guiding her to illustrate my story. I can enjoy the happy surprises when she returns with sketches that improve upon my initial ideas!

Now is your opportunity to pull all this together (and write your answers in your personal journal):

Momentum Action Plan (MAP) — so far
- What do you want?
- No. Come on, what do you really want?
- Better yet, what do you want to feel and note your impressions of See, Hear and Touch.
- How can you experience the heart (core elements/the heart of the matter) on a small scale?

A Special Note about What You Want

When you consider what you want, take a moment to put aside your thoughts and feelings that hold you back — like putting them into a drawer. Imagine that the Genie from *Aladdin* is here. You can have anything you want if you just write the details into your Momentum Action Plan.

My point is that once you voice what you want to feel and write it out where you can see it, you have made a major leap forward toward getting what you want.

Unfortunately, many of us will need to counteract our impulses to guard against disappointment and to avoid wanting too much. Please know that life brings disappointment no matter what. Playing small does not safeguard us from experiencing disappointment. But playing small does prevent us from enjoying surges of excitement and feelings of fulfillment that come with pursuing our dreams.

On the other hand, things flow better when you allow yourself to imagine big possibilities, and the universe provides you with some terrific, surprise opportunities. For example, years ago, as I walked down the corridors of the university I graduated from, I had a sudden feeling of *I want to teach*. Later, the father of one of the actors in a feature film

I was directing alerted me to film-related group and website. Through that website, I learned of a possible teaching position at a particular college. At the time of this writing I have been teaching graduate students and college students for over 16 years.

The point of this story is to get in touch with what you want. When you do, you open the door to joyful possibilities.

Now, we are ready for the next question ...

Momentum Action Plan (MAP)
Question 5: How can you graduate up levels?
First, let's look at an example of my client who wants to be an actor. As a novice actor, she can:
- Take an acting class.
- Participate in Community Theater.
- Get a headshot (photo) made.
- Audition for local commercials.
- Make her own digital film that she can edit using her home computer. Or she can utilize the filmmaking talents of students at a local college.

Someone starting a business can plan out the steps needed to achieve a goal—that is, climb up a step and graduate to the next level. Let's say this person wants to become a professional speaker who sells products on the Internet.

She can:
- *Level One:* Give a free talk to a local association. Record the talk with a video camera and attach a microphone to her collar for the audio component.
- *Level Two:* Take the audio recording from the speech and download it onto a home computer. Make three copies of the speech by recording it

onto CDs.
- *Level Two (part 2):* Take the three CDs to the next speech she gives to see if they sell.
- *Level Three:* Make more copies if the initial three CDs sell.
- *Level Four:* Consider writing a book based on the topic of the CDs she has been selling.
- *Level Five:* Write a book proposal to submit to an agent (who will submit it to a publisher).
- *Level Five (alterative):* Self-publish the book.

A person who self-publishes his or her first book is in good company: Deepak Chopra, Edgar Allen Poe, Sigmund Freud and many others have done just that. In fact, author Christopher Paolini, when he was 19-years-old (and with his parents' help), self-published the book *Eragon*. This book was made into a major motion picture.

The idea is to rise upward step by step. The question is *How can you graduate up levels?* If you don't know what the levels are, you can get a coach or listen to educational audio programs. Also, review your answers to Questions 1 through 4 to help you understand what you truly want, and your feelings about those desires. Then create a concise plan that will help you reach your next levels.

In order to make progress you need to stretch your comfort zone a little. But the important thing is to ease into doing new activities, which is covered in our next section ...

Momentum Action Plan (MAP)
Question 6: How can you gain an Immediate Victory?
The process for picking something that will be your Immediate Victory begins with preparation. Begin by writing down three easy things that will lead you in the direction of what you want. Make sure they're easy.

My clients have written:
- Do a Google search on the topic I'm interested in.
- Go to the bookstore and browse the books related to what I'm interested in.
- Get the book and read it for 15 minutes.

The Immediate Victory is a two-fold strategy: Focus on your successful action and then reward yourself for your accomplishment.

When you begin with easy victories and rewards, you feel encouraged to progress toward your goal.

During one interview, the host of a show said her reward was chocolate.

"I suggest that you have a menu."

"Of chocolate?" she replied, with humor.

I'm suggesting various rewards—and definitely some that don't involve calories.

In addition to writing down three easy tasks, write the rewards you want—so you have something to anticipate.

Rewards my clients have written include:
- A hot bath
- A phone call with my best friend
- To read my favorite fiction book
- To listen to an MP3 of my favorite singer

A reward is a wonderful way to encourage you to take more and more steps toward your goal. Starting with something easy prevents you from procrastinating. Researchers note that procrastination comes from fear and the anticipation of pain. Taking easy steps first helps eliminate both fear and concerns about pain.

Ease Into Momentum by starting with something easy. Reward yourself for your success. When you do your inner child says: "YES! This is great. I'll give you the energy to do more of this."

Your inner child is the part of you that feels small and vulnerable and wants to play. I emphasize that a strategy of Emotional Leverage is to make space to take care of your inner child. Find ways to be good to yourself and to include fun as part of your day.

Momentum helps you keep going. *You free yourself for success when you Ease Into Momentum.*

I call this process *The Easy Part Start.* If you want to write a book, you can start with an easy task: writing the chapter titles. That's what I do. Then I make a list of my anecdotes and a specific detail of research for each chapter.

The idea is to take action. Stop talking, and start doing.

Mother Teresa said, "There should be less talk; a preaching point is not a meeting point. What do you do then? Take a broom and clean someone's house. That says enough."

We are inspired to take a small step forward—The Easy Part Start. This reminds me of the old phrase: To know and not to do, is not to know. Let's take action … and move on to the next question.

Momentum Action Plan (MAP)
Question 7: How can you announce what you offer?

Focusing on this question "How can you tell the world what you offer?" is a crucial step that many people leave out. There are those who would rather keep their heads down and just do their work. A number of artists and engineering-type people would prefer a world in which they just do a good job—and hope magically to get rewarded. But it doesn't work that way. People need to see you doing quality work.

In order to make your dreams come true you need to tell the world what you offer. And, the essence of telling the world is to clearly and concisely express what you're best known for. This is your personal brand.

The center of personal branding is this question, *"What am I best known for?*

When I think of *what am I best known for?* I think of this story Sam told in a job interview:

"I was hired to be a unit production manager for a feature film. The screenplay called for a bus. But the budget was strained. We needed a public place so that the romantic leads could meet by happenstance. A bus would require rental fees, hiring an off-duty police officer, hiring a bunch of extras, feeding everyone, and getting costly permits. I suggested the solution of having the two people meet in an elevator. Then I suggested that we could build an inexpensive elevator set in a living room using two by fours. The face of the producer lit up with relief. She told me, "Sam, I can always count on you to solve a problem with creativity and to guard the budget. Good work."

So what do you think Sam is best known for? The answer is in the producer's comment. In essence, Sam solves problems with creativity and he guards the budget.

Sharing a story illustrates a desired characteristic, and this is a vital part of your personal brand.

Here are the elements of your personal brand:
- The answer to "what am I best known for?"
- A story that moves emotions
- A label
- A soundbite

Here's how Sam's might fill in his personal brand elements:

What am I best known for?

Solving problems with creativity and guarding the budget.

A story that moves emotions
Sam solves the problem for completing the feature film.
A label
Sam is a creative solution finder.
A soundbite
"Sam, I can always count on you to solve a problem with creativity and to guard the budget."

Find ways to effectively show what you offer. That's what Elijah Wood did when he wanted to play Frodo in the feature film trilogy *The Lord Of The Rings*. He had a friend videotape him wearing Hobbit clothes and doing an English accent. Elijah sent the videotape to the director Peter Jackson. That's how Elijah Wood came to star in the world-famous epic. By the way, *The Lord of the Rings III: The Return of the King* is the first fantasy movie in history to win Best Picture at the Academy Awards!

Remember that other people may influence the things you want:
- There's a job you want.
- There's funding you want.
- There's a movie role you want.

You need to effectively tell people what you offer.

That's the magic of an effective personal brand. Here are examples:
- My personal brand is Tom Marcoux, Executive Coach and Spoken Word Strategist
- Tony Robbins calls himself America's Results Coach.
- Mark Victor Hansen uses the phrase America's Ambassador of Possibility.

An effective personal brand works in job interviews.

In a job interview, one of my clients used the phrase: "At XY Company, I was the go-to person for computers."

A personal brand makes you memorable. In a job interview a person could say: "I was called the Captain of Cost-cutting."

The idea is to give the interviewer the words she will repeat to her colleagues.

The interviewer will say, "Yes, Janet Smith is impressive. You know, she was known as the Captain of Cost-cutting at XY Company."

A personal brand involves a powerful story that moves emotions. For a job interview, plan to tell a story about how you saved the day using your skills or talents.

A personal brand quickly helps people get to know and trust you. It makes you stand out from other people.

Your personal brand improves your website.

On a number of occasions, I help my clients create a powerful personal brand that they present on their websites. [For example, I helped one client start from zero and then have visitors (from *173 countries*) to her blog.] I teach them to design their websites to provide visitors with a quick overview of who they are and what their services provide.

Websites need to answer the following questions that a web visitor has:
- *Question 1:* Who are you?
- *Question 2:* How can you help me?
- *Question 3:* How can you show you me that you're an expert?
- *Question 4:* How can you show me that you're trustworthy?
- *Question 5:* Why must I take action now? (It's best when you design a hyperlink that entices the web visitor to click immediately.)

Researchers have noted that people decide to leave a website within four seconds after arriving on a webpage—if their interest isn't grabbed immediately. Webmasters need to seize the attention of the web visitor. The above questions help them improve the design of their website—and attract visitors who will stay longer than four seconds. In the Internet world, establishing a personal brand is how to gain the visitor's trust and the person's business. In this way, prosperity can be expanded.

Here's another example of a personal brand: Tom Marcoux, The Personal Branding Instructor, as identified by *The San Francisco Examiner*. This example, which gives much more information about me, is almost similar to an endorsement.

Your personal brand needs to be true.

You need to be able to back up your personal brand with expertise. For example, my website has the domain name TomSuperCoach.com. When I started using that domain name I knew my friends and colleagues in the speaking industry would tease me about it. And they did send emails teasingly addressed to "Hey SuperCoach." Or, "Hello SuperTom."

There is a solution to the teasing: Live up to your personal brand. My domain name, TomSuperCoach.com, has proven to work because:

- I study every day.
- I put in significant effort to provide helpful, effective coaching to my clients.
- I have a track record of guiding clients, audiences and readers to great results for over two decades.

Another point is the domain name of TomSuperCoach.com solves an important problem when I appear on television and radio. One TV host asked, "How does our audience get in contact with you?" When I replied "TomMarcoux.com," the host asked, "How do you spell

Marcoux?" This is why my team came up with TomSuperCoach.com.

Problem solved, and a personal brand was created.

[Additionally, I invite people to visit my blog at YourBodySoulandProsperity.com.]

Your personal brand is the method to effectively tell the world what you offer.

Momentum Action Plan (MAP)

Question 8: Say: "I want <goal> & my obstacle is <impediment>"

In my workshops, I hear audience members say:
- I want to start a business, but my obstacle is no money.
- I want to act and win an Oscar award, but my obstacle is I don't know anyone in the movie industry.

In some of my speeches I show a graphic with a STOP sign. I change it into a START sign with just three letters: A-R-T. The art of making a breakthrough is to connect with people, ask questions, and get new ideas.

Now it's your turn. Fill in the blanks and write this down:
I want <goal or desire> and my obstacle [to getting what I want] is <impediment>.

The idea is to talk to people about your goal—after you have taken some action steps in the right direction.

When you talk about your goal, you might hear someone say something like: "Oh, my cousin Stephen is an agent in Los Angeles."

One interviewer asked me, "How can I tell people what I want and the obstacle in front of it without sounding desperate?" I replied, "It's a matter of tone and timing. First, you listen to the other person. When you're listening, you're making rapport. Then, when the person asks 'What do you do?' you can reply with something like, 'At the moment, I'm a teacher. But what I'm really focusing on is moving my writing career forward. My obstacle is that I'm looking for a literary agent."

Here is an example of how connecting with one person can blossom into a big opportunity. When I began making films, many years ago, I didn't know anyone. To get started in the industry, I wrote a screenplay that I showed to a software engineer who passed it to another engineer. It then went to a real estate developer and finally to the California Motion Picture Commissioner. Three years later, when I directed my first feature film, the California Motion Picture Commissioner became my Associate Producer. He secured for me an airport and airplane—for free—for the film's production.

Remember to prepare so you can clearly express:

I want <goal or desire> and my obstacle [to getting what I want] is <impediment>.

Momentum Action Plan (MAP)

Question 9: Ask, "Give me suggestions, leads, wild ideas?"

To ask for suggestions, leads and wild ideas is an important part of getting a breakthrough. We need to get new ideas. We need the input of other people.

Participants in my workshops and seminars learn powerful ideas by sharing with each other.

Ask for input or feedback. *Ask someone. Ask Higher Power.*

The next process is something that I teach to my college students. I use a process I call *Choice Market Testing*™.

To get productive feedback, show someone two versions of something you're working on and ask these two questions

in this sequence:
1. Which one do you prefer?
2. What about <the person's preference> grabs your attention?

Ask for help from Higher Power.

Jack Canfield came up with the title for his bestselling series *Chicken Soup for the Soul* by asking for God's help. He asked God to awaken him the next morning with bestselling titles. He woke up with the phrase "Chicken Soup for the Spirit" in his mind.

Remember to ask for help. A number of millionaires have said, "Wealth is a team sport."

Momentum Action Plan (MAP)
Question 10: Write due dates next to items on your list

We have now come to the final step in your Momentum Action Plan: Write a due date next to important items on your MAP. This is crucial. Remember this old phrase: A goal without a due date is just a wish.

This reminds me of a time when I was directing a feature film. When I'm directing a feature film, believe me, I'm under timeline constraints.

Here's the situation: I am on the set when a little 8-year-old actress, Kim, is expected to arrive at any moment. While I'm talking with my director of photography, a crew member calls out, "Kim's here."

I turn around, and my jaw hits the floor. There is Kim, with her timid little smile and a HUGE cast on her thumb. Broken thumbs were not in the script! So I tell everyone to Take 5, which means five minutes. I really want to say take five hours because I don't know what to do. So I sit down to rewrite the script. I immediately stand up and pace—trying to figure out what to do. After a while I come up with an idea.

I call the cast and crew to the set. The rewritten scene includes two brothers talking to each other. One brother is the father of Kim's character. The father had left the little girl in the care of his older brother. The older brother, disgusted with his brother's unchecked alcoholism, says, "Just in case you're interested, Kim broke her thumb!" Furious, the father pulls his fist back to slug his brother. Of course, the father is interested in his daughter's health! Just then Kim runs in, broken thumb and all, and says, "Daddy!"

I was relieved that my quick solution made the film better. When making a film, the director needs to adhere to a budget and schedule. In essence, the director has a due date every day in that a certain number of scenes must be filmed each day.

Having a due date makes you get creative. It helps you charge up with energy.

* * *

By filling in the details of the Momentum Action Plan (MAP), you have gone through the 9-Minute Miracle Breakthrough—although the training process probably took more than nine minutes. However, going forward, now that you know the process you can complete the Momentum Action

Plan for your week or month in nine minutes or less. You can make copies of the blank Momentum Action Plan form, which appears after the filled-in example (see the next few pages).

Momentum Action Plan (MAP)
(An example)

1. What do you want?

To complete my children's book which will lead to an

animated feature film.

2. No. Come on, what do you really want?

To uplift the lives of millions of people in ways similar to what Walt Disney did.

3. Better yet, what do you want to feel?

See: The smiling faces of an audience watching the animated film I directed.

Hear: The applause of an audience during the closing credits of the film.

Touch: To shake hands with people who buy the children's book that accompanies the film.

I want to feel really alive. I want to feel the exuberance when audience members laugh while watching my animated feature film.

4. How can you experience the HEART (core elements/the heart of the matter) on a small scale?

The heart of the matter is to enjoy the excitement of collaboration—when people come together and make a "whole" that is better than the sum of the parts. I can enjoy the process of working with the artist, and guiding her to illustrate my story. I can enjoy the happy surprises when she returns with sketches that improve upon my initial ideas!

5. How can you graduate up levels?

Level One: Complete my children's book and make 25 copies.

Level Two: Obtain an agent and seek a publisher to publish a version of my book on a massive scale.

Level Three: Prepare for an animated feature—including storyboards and a budget.

Level Four: Seek to expand my circle of contacts and leads.

6. How can you do something easy and gain an Immediate Victory?

Go to Amazon.com and find a book on preparing an

animated feature film. My reward can be an hour in a warm bath with soothing music.

7. How can you tell the world what you offer? (personal branding)

Come up with a soundbite to describe the children's book. Come up with a memorable domain name.

8. Say: "I want <goal or desire> and my obstacle is <impediment>." (Tell someone.)

I want to produce and direct an animated feature film. My obstacle is to find funding sources.

9. Ask: "Please give me suggestions, leads, and wild ideas." (Ask someone. Ask Higher Power.)

Contact an association that supports uplifting media projects and ask them for the names of people who help film projects gain funding and support.

10. Write a due date next to an item on your list.

On March 19, 20__, I will contact the media association toward gaining contacts and leads.

* * * * * *

Momentum Action Plan (MAP)

To help you stay on track, complete this process on a weekly or monthly basis.

1. What do you want?

2. No. Come on, what do you really want?

3. Better yet, what do you want to feel?
See:
Hear:
Touch:

4. How can you experience the HEART (core elements/the heart of the matter) on a small scale?

5. How can you graduate up levels?

6. How can you do something easy and gain an Immediate Victory?

7. How can you tell the world what you offer? (personal branding)

8. Say: "I want <goal or desire> and my obstacle is <impediment>." (Tell someone.)

9. Ask: "Please give me suggestions, leads, and wild ideas." (Ask someone. Ask Higher Power.)

10. Write a due date next to an item on your list.

Copyright Tom Marcoux   YourBodySoulandProsperity.com

**Here is a principle for your *Year of Awesome*:
Principle #3: Concentrate on *Top Six Targets***

Power Question: How will you record your Top Six Targets each day (3x5 card, journal, Smartphone)?

April – April Showers

"April showers bring May flowers"
– traditional saying in English speaking countries

Two thoughts arise for me: a) you need to nurture in April to get blossoms in May and b) to have a harvest, you'll need to endure some discomfort.

That means you need to sow the seeds of well-being.

"I'm afraid that I can't keep up this pace," my new client Sharon said. Being an entrepreneur was new for her, and she was afraid of burning out.

"An important part of our process is going to be helping you get stronger. We need you to have 'reserves,'" I said.

"Reserves of what?"

"Let me ask you. What do you need?" I asked.

"Need? Some time off. Some sleep. Some peace of mind," Sharon said.

"Good. That's the place to start."

Principle #4: Create your "reserves."

"Build a superreserve in every area: have more than enough."
– Thomas Leonard

The protective wall to your personal energy is made of your superreserves. Creating conditions for enough sleep, appropriate nutrition, excellent daily exercise will not arise by themselves. You must devote purposeful attention.

How?

Keep what I call a Self-Leadership Chart.

Note your most important daily activities. For example, I log my sleep. When I miss sleep on a particular night, I juggle my schedule over the next days to do better in that category.

"I will do today what others will not do, so tomorrow I can do what others cannot do." – Randy Gage

Take excellent care of yourself. That's unusual in today's society. Look around and you'll see people abusing their bodies—their only home on the planet.

So take action and create reserves of personal energy and inner calm.

Here is a principle for your *Year of Awesome*:
Principle #4: Create your "reserves."

Power Question: How will you take action TODAY toward building up your reserves of personal energy and inner calm?

May – May the Force Be With You

"May the 4th be with you" (signifying Star Wars Day) comes to mind. The actual phrase is: "May the Force be with you" (expressed in *Star Wars: Episode IV: A New Hope*—the first one filmed and released in 1977).

We learn, in dialogue, that the Force has a Light Side and a Dark Side:

"For my ally is the Force, and a powerful ally it is. Life creates it, makes it grow. Its energy surrounds us and binds us. Luminous beings are we, not this crude matter. You must feel the Force around you; here, between you, me, the tree, the rock, everywhere, yes. Even between the land and the ship." – Yoda, STAR WARS: EPISODE V: THE EMPIRE STRIKES BACK

"Yes, a Jedi's strength flows from the Force. But beware of the dark side. Anger, fear, aggression; the dark side of the Force are they. Easily they flow, quick to join you in a fight. If once you start down the dark path, forever will it dominate your destiny, consume you it will, as it did Obi-Wan's apprentice." – Yoda

The idea of a dark side and a light side resonates with something uncovered by researchers.

It turns out that our brain has a "dark side." That is, any negative experience goes straight into our long-term memory.

On the other hand, **any positive experience requires at least 10 seconds of focused attention** to get said experience into our long-term memory.

What is the consequence of this? In a few words: Many of us live most of our day in the clutches of the dark and negative. Ask someone how her day is, she is likely to respond with complaints. Why? Because the negative experiences are truly vivid. It's the power of the "dark side."

Here is the next principle for your *Year of Awesome:*

Principle #5: Energize "10 Seconds to Wealth"

In 10 seconds you can close a sale or begin a healthy new relationship. On the other hand, in 10 seconds you can torpedo that sale or new relationship.

The point is this: Condition yourself to be ready for those all-important 10 seconds—that window of opportunity when you can make a difference.

For instance, we all know the importance of the first 10 seconds when meeting someone new. After all, first impressions last a long time. However, life changes when we least expect it.

Those all-important 10 seconds can come at any time. Always be prepared for whatever might come next.

Do you realize you have hidden gifts that can help you in those crucial 10 seconds? You can:

- Keep your cool in a negotiation or other sensitive situations.
- Feel deep fulfillment and happiness in the moment.
- Inspire good feelings in a friend, colleague or romantic partner.

Recent research has revealed how the brain processes input.

We have learned:

- Successful entrepreneurs interpret situations differently than other people.

- Successful salespeople can envision the sale before making an important sales call.
- People who enjoy warm relationships know how to help others feel heard and cared for.

The point is:

Oftentimes, 10 seconds can be crucial to the outcome of any situation!

Have you noticed that in 10 seconds you can do something powerful? You can:

- Say something that makes a friend feel important.
- Lose your temper and say something that you'll regret.
- Calm yourself down to make a situation better.

* * * * * *

10 Seconds to Wealth

The essence is this:

- In 10 seconds you can close a sale or torpedo a relationship.
- Using your Divine Gifts (covered in an earlier section of this book) enables you to be at your best during the crucial 10 seconds of any interaction — whether those 10 seconds are at the beginning, middle or end of the interaction.
- 10 seconds may be what's needed to build and enhance positive connections with the people who are the keys to your success and fulfillment.
- The strategy is to condition yourself to be at your best during those all-important 10 seconds (This book includes many methods to achieve that strategy).
- Recent brain research notes that it takes 10 seconds for positive input to impact your long-term memory. This means that memorizing

empowering thoughts, rehearsing effective behaviors, and writing positive details in your personal journal all help to physically alter your brain so that it is inclined toward the positive.
- Conditioning yourself for positive change helps you overcome your "default settings."*

[* A default setting is something that has been programmed into you at some point in your past. People tend to fall back to their default setting when under stress. For example, people who become extremely nervous when delivering a speech may have had a traumatic experience giving a presentation at some point in the past.]

* * * * * *

Scientists confirm that you can condition yourself to be positive. How? Through what scientists call "brain plasticity," which refers to the ability of the brain to change as a result of one's experience (the brain is "plastic" and "malleable"). We'll discuss this idea later in more detail.

We'll begin with belly breathing

Here is a simple process to help your mind and body experience peace. Breathe in through your nose while allowing your belly to expand. Hold your breath for a moment, and then breathe out through your mouth while letting your belly to get smaller. Repeat this process ten times. How do you feel now? My clients have reported feeling relaxed and even stronger.

Now imagine practicing belly breathing every day. What happens? You condition your mind and body to experience inner peace. Augment belly breathing with meditation. In its simplest form, you merely sit quietly for six minutes and focus only on your breath flowing in and out. No strain. No effort.

Research has shown that people can learn to be positive in much the same way one learns to play an instrument. Neuroscientists Antoine Lutz and Richard Davidson found that people who regularly meditate could physically change their brains. The scientists used fMRIs and EEGs to study how a meditator's brain functions differently. They found that brain circuits used to detect emotions and feelings were dramatically changed in those who meditate regularly.

10 seconds are crucial to long-term memory.
Psychologist Rick Hanson and neurologist Richard Mendius wrote about how the brain is hard-wired to scan for the bad. They note: "Positive experiences are usually registered through standard memory systems, and thus need to be held in conscious awareness for ten to twenty seconds for them to really sink in."

The point here is that you need to condition your brain to be at your best during the crucial 10 seconds of interaction with a client, co-worker or loved one.

Condition your brain to be inclined toward the positive.
People in the habit of regularly writing in a journal about what is going well in their lives actually experience more happiness.

For years I have written in my *Daily Journal of Victories and Blessings,* and I feel grateful and happy when it's time for sleep. Researchers have discovered that journal writing makes it easier for many people to fall asleep. I invite you to begin this healthy habit tonight.

Psychologists Robert Emmons and Michael McCullough verified the value of writing in a gratitude journal. Their study revealed that a group of people writing five things for which they were grateful "ended up happier, much more optimistic about the future and physically healthier—and they even exercised more."*

[* Research on the benefits of keeping a gratitude journal was reported in the book *59 Seconds: Think a Little, Change a Lot* by Richard Wiseman.]

Remember that you can condition yourself to stay "on the Light Side of the Force" or at least "the positive side of your brain."

As a side note: Here are a couple of comments from George Lucas, creator of *Star Wars:*

"I thought Star Wars *was too wacky for the general public."*
– George Lucas

"The secret is not to give up hope. It's very hard not to because if you're really doing something worthwhile I think you will be pushed to the brink of hopelessness before you come through the other side." – George Lucas

It's interesting that the first film released in 1977 has come to be known as *Star Wars: Episode IV: A New Hope.*

George has expressed some essential truth. Even though he had some doubts about whether *Star Wars* would gain mass popularity, George still held to the hope that he was making something that would touch some people's hearts.

It's a joy to see that George's hope continues to this day and as a source of inspiration for today's generation.

For your *Year of Awesome:*
Principle #5: Energize "10 Seconds to Wealth"
Power Questions: Will you practice deep breathing to condition yourself to calm down? Will you write in a *Daily Journal of Victories and Blessings* to condition yourself to focus

on positive events in your life?

June – June Weddings

When I looked up "June" I found a lot of comments about June Weddings.

I'm not going into the historical details about the Roman Goddess Juno and how she is considered the protector of women, and in particular, in marriage and childbearing—and how world cultures liked the idea that women would be available to help with the harvest—after bearing a child. (Oh, I did share some details.)

I'm thinking about weddings and commitment.

Let's face it: Commitment is less scary when you really want something!

Some years ago, I wrote about **"freedom through commitment."** In this context, commitment is NOT chains; instead it is a path. You become free to experience true love, loyalty, persistence, compassion and strength.

Principle #6: Succeed through commitment to "the pipeline and better-than-zero"

Commitment to "Always be filling the pipeline"

Salespeople refer to the pipeline. This is a metaphor that one may place oil at the head of a pipeline, but it takes a significant amount of time before the oil arrives at the other end of the pipeline. In few words, this means that one needs to connect with new prospective customers daily—because it will take a significant amount of time and effort to close some sales.

"As an example, I might be raising money for a new business

idea .... I'll most likely be speaking to twenty-five to fifty investors who are each capable of writing the check I need. And I'll have twenty-five more in the pipeline as backups in case the first fifty fall through." – Wayne Allen Root

I learned about this process the hard way. One time I was helping someone, "Nick" and through my coaching he was already getting great results at his fast-paced tech company. When I specifically invited him to become my client, he said, "No. Thank you. Not at this time." This hurt.

I said to my sweetheart:

"If you have one, and one says 'no,' it's a tragedy.
If you have 20, and one says 'no,' it's just a step."

So since that time, I have devoted much more attention and effort to filling the pipeline with at least 20 if not more people. This takes focus and setting personal quotas.

Commitment to "Better Than Zero"

Taking one small, positive action is better than doing nothing. That's the inspiration for my phrase: "Better than zero."

On numerous occasions, I've invited my sweetheart to take a 15-minute walk after we've returned from an evening event. Why? It's "Better than zero." Furthermore, it "keeps us in practice." We acquired the habit of taking a daily walk—no matter what.

Here is a principle for your *Year of Awesome:*

Principle #6: Succeed through commitment to "the pipeline and better-than-zero"

Power Question: How will you place daily actions into your schedule? What will you commit to? If you're a business owner, will you commit to making at least 5

marketing phone calls a day (or some other marketing actions)?

July – 4th of July

July 4th in the United States is a holiday commemorating the adoption of the *Declaration of Independence* in 1776 by the Continental Congress.

Here's something truly helpful: **Declare that you're in a new chapter of life—starting now!**

Why? When you declare your new chapter of life, you choose what you want to be in your life from this moment forward and what you want to eliminate from your daily experience.

Principle #7: Sort and Declare a New Chapter of Life

When I say "sort," I mean take a good look at the elements of your life. Are you wasting time with certain people? Are you looking for support from certain people who cannot give it?

I've learned the hard way that some friends will not come with you as you step into a new chapter of your life. If you really express your natural talents and you have "home runs" where you serve lots of people, an old friend may start to feel uncomfortable around you.

Years ago, I had a particular friend who would be harsh in his criticism of my work and actions. I sensed something and told this friend the truth: "I'm concerned that when I have a home run and a project brings in real prosperity, you're going to make up a reason and get mad at me. And then go away."

I was surprised that the guy said *nothing*. And he did

choose to leave my life. I grieved over the loss.

Still, I have discovered that I have more personal energy now with him *not* in my life. His absence and the saving in time and energy have been so helpful.

There's an old phrase: Some people brighten a room by leaving it.

So use the following questions below to sort what you want in your life and what you want to be *the special parts of your New Chapter of Life.*

Here is a principle for your *Year of Awesome:*
Principle #7: Sort and Declare a New Chapter of Life

Power Questions: What unhealthy activities (and even friendships) will you now drop from your life? What do you want this New Chapter of Life to be about? What do you now value the most? How will you support yourself to keep to your new practices and actions in Your New Chapter of Life?

August – Friendship Day

When I did a Google search about August, I found "Friendship day (first Sunday of August)."

The relates to …

Principle #8: Act to support friendships.

I always remember this quote from W. H. Auden: "Among those whom I like or admire, I can find no common denominator, but among those whom I love, I can: all of them make me laugh."

It's valuable to learn to make room for laughter and warmth in your friendships and other relationships.

Prosperity is Founded on Relationships
Great Relationships Expand Financial Abundance

In this section, we focus on how to build and warm up your relationships through inspiring humor and laughter.

Enhancing relationships helps create the opportunities for the wealth you desire. Humor is an important component. "Laughter is the closest distance between two people," said comedian Victor Borge.

The important thing to realize is this: *Real financial abundance is built on great relationships.* We often hear about the "big break," and many times that opportunity comes from a good relationship established years earlier. When you are committed to expanding prosperity, you are committed to improving your relationship-building skills. Here's an example:

On the set of a major motion picture, the Assistant Director was sweating bullets. Any delay meant $100,000 was being lost in wages, equipment rental and crew salaries. The Assistant Director turned to his crew members and, in a light tone, said, "Come on guys, let's pick it up a bit. You've got me looking at the Want Ads." The crew members moved faster, and the filming day was saved. Just the right tone and humorous words did the trick.

Learning to add humor helps you:

1. *Lead a team.* To create more abundance, we often find that we must become a leader of a team. "A sense of humor is part of the art of leadership, of getting along with people, of getting things done," said President Dwight D. Eisenhower.
2. *Inspire people.* Leaders need to inspire people. Great leaders use humor to build a community. "Laughter is the sun that drives winter from the human face," wrote statesman and novelist Victor Hugo.
3. *Improve your daily life.* "Humor is the great thing, the saving thing. The minute it crops up, all our irritations and resentments slip away and a sunny spirit takes their place," wrote Mark Twain.
4. *Enjoy giving and receiving love.* "We cannot really love anybody with whom we never laugh," noted writer Agnes Repplier.
5. *Diffuse anger.* "You cannot be mad at somebody who makes you laugh—it's as simple as that," said Jay Leno.
6. *Become resilient.* "Life is tough, and if you have the ability to laugh at it you have the ability to enjoy it," said Salma Hayek. Also, Albert Camus wrote, "In the depth of winter I finally learned that there

was in me an invincible summer."
7. *Create a spiritual connection with people.* "Among those whom I like or admire, I can find no common denominator, but among those whom I love, I can: all of them make me laugh," emphasized poet W. H. Auden.

We can communicate well and create warmth in our relationships when we use humor to support our efforts. Often we hear, "She was a great speaker." Why? "Because she was funny, and she told great stories."

Here are methods to help you use humor. Humor is not merely telling jokes. Often, humor arises when emphasizing certain details in a story. Human beings are built to appreciate stories. An old phrase holds: "God created people because God wanted to hear stories." This chapter is based on my presentation, *Get Connected through Humor*.

Appropriate humor can warm up and deepen a relationship. We use the H.U.M.O.R. process:

H – Honor the personality style
U – Understand that no humor bit works for everyone
M – Mirror the person's humor preference
O – Open the door
R – Respect the person and environment

H—Honor the personality style

Our goal is to create rapport with other people. Before you use certain humor-creating methods, note the personality style of the person you are addressing. Here is an example of a behavior to avoid:

One time at an office supply store, the clerk made a client Stephen wait for a while, and then short-changed him. The manager was nearby and said, "Oh, that's how we get the money to order lunch." His attempt at humor completely broke a possible rapport with Stephen. Neither the clerk nor manager said, "I'm sorry for causing you inconvenience." That would have been appreciated because Stephen was under a deadline and lots of pressure. It would have been better if the manager had been respectful during their first encounter. Although his attempt at humor might have been well-intended, the manager's method of handling the situation was not appreciated. It would have been better to begin with an apology.

U—Understand that no humor bit works for everyone

No item of humor works on all people. It helps to have ways to bounce back when the humor does not work. For example, once when speaking to over 300 people, I made a comment: "I wonder how Captain Kirk would handle this. Mr. Spock, raise the 'stress' shields." Some laughter. Still, I felt that my humor bit missed the mark. Then I said, "I guess that one was for the Trekkies." More laughter. That saved the moment. I generated two moments of laughter.*

[*Yes, I know that Star Trek fans prefer the term "Trekkers." For non-fans and to facilitate the humor bit, I had to use the other word.]

M—Mirror the person's humor preference

Roger Dawson, author of *The Secrets of Power Persuasion*, identifies five patterns of humor. I will supply my example for each pattern:

- *Exaggeration:* A friend told me about a time when she was staying in a particular apartment building. She told someone: 'If these cockroaches get any bigger, I'll have to put them on a leash!'
- *Putdowns:* "And then Joe said, 'A martial artist? He couldn't kung-fu his way out of a paper bag!'" (I personally avoid putdown humor because it can

cause trouble and hurt feelings.)
- *Puns:* I stand at work. The agony of the feet. (defeat)
- *Silliness:* In *The Pink Panther*, Peter Sellers does pratfalls.
- *Surprise:* Henny Youngman said, "Take my wife—please!"

Listen to the other person's preferences in humor. I have a friend who is a software engineer, and he loves wordplay. He is the only person I share puns with.

O—Open the door
Listen carefully to how the other person responds to something with a humorous tint. To open the door to humor: In the beginning, try small, gentle humor items. Perhaps, you might share an innocent cartoon from a local newspaper. See if the person chuckles, smiles, or fails to respond.

R—Respect the person and environment
I advise against using profanity. To many people, the only sure-fire environment where profanity usually fits in is a standup comedy nightclub. When using profanity outside a nightclub, be sensitive about the environment and the personalities that are present.

30 Secrets for Creating Humor
Secret 1: Prepare the Stage
In my college classes, I say a few things to help the students realize that appropriate humor will be part of my presentations. I mention that "humor will walk into the class at times, and go running out."

Secret 2: Notice that timing is acquired through practice

The secret to creating humor is to practice on safe audiences. Practice your humor on your loved ones and friends. Choose someone with whom you have a high comfort level. It is helpful to practice because successful expressions of humor require smoothness and comfort on your part.

Secret 3: Gain timing through subconscious modeling

We learned to talk through subconscious modeling when we heard our parents talk. Through them we modeled our behaviors.

Now the question is this: How do you get comedic timing working for you subconsciously? Learn from stand-up comedians and by watching romantic comedy movies. When you're watching and enjoying these programs, you are subconsciously modeling the behavior of the comedians.

Secret 4: Play with words

When I visited the Comedy Warehouse in Walt Disney World, I witnessed comedians making up improvised humor. A comedian interviewed an audience member who met her fiancée through the Internet. The comedy troupe sang songs with these phrases:
- In Amsterdam — we'll go Dutch.
- She caught him in her net (Internet)
- You got a male (you got mail)

Secret 5: Use a good setup

At the Comedy Warehouse, the comedy troupe sang improvised songs. We, the audience, were told that the performance was improvised. However, as a comedy writer, I could see the pre-set structures. The performers knew certain music passages. The piano player had to know the pre-set song patterns. Also, the performers were using certain preset rhythms that I'm sure they practiced and rehearsed. Still, the audience laughed more and more because it was set up to believe that the performers were performing without a net.

Secret 6: Base humor on a song pattern

Some years ago, a friend and I waited and waited for a table at a restaurant. We were starving. I remembered the song by the rock band, Queen: "We will, we will rock you." Then, I sang to my friend, "We will, we will grovel!" I mimed begging for food.

Secret 7: Create a running joke based on the situation

In the situation when my friend and I were starving and waiting at the particular restaurant, I created three spontaneous bits of humor. The running joke was being hungry. The humor came from my voicing some exaggerated reactions to the hunger.

Secret 8: Base humor on icons, like *Star Wars*

While starving and waiting at the restaurant, I reminded my friend of a situation in *Star Wars: Episode IV: A New Hope* (the first film released in 1977). Obi-wan Kenobi, the Jedi Knight, had used the Force to change people's minds. He said, "These aren't the 'droids you're looking for." Succumbing to Obi-Wan's power, the Stormtrooper replied, "Uh, these aren't the 'droids we're looking for."

Since my friend and I were still waiting to be served lunch, I made the connection that we wanted the waiter (like a hypnotized Stormtrooper) to bring us our food. I said (like I was Obi-wan Kenobi): "You want to bring Tom and Sarah the food right now." Then, I said, like I was the waiter, "Oh, we're bringing the food right now." And the food arrived within seconds!

Secret 9: Enjoy understatement

At Walt Disney World, I watched a film about the art of animation. One animator who was balding and round said,

"I was given Phil (in *Hercules*) to animate. He's short. He's bald. He's kind of fat. It's a stretch for me." Laughter rose from the audience. It was a triumph of understatement.

Secret 10: Tie-in experiences shared by the audience

At the Comedy Warehouse at Walt Disney World, a woman hesitated giving a book to a comedian. The comedian said, "You've got to give it back. There's nothing free at Disney." The crowd roared with laughter.

Secret 11: Choose a good target (perhaps yourself)

Denis Waitley, the best-selling author of *The Psychology of Winning*, uses himself as the target of humor. He speaks about the missteps he took when young and caught up in his ego. He talks about when he was a fighter pilot. He says, "I mowed the lawn in my flight suit—so the neighbors knew who they were living next to."

Secret 12: Remember to use context well

"There's nothing free at Disney" works so well because the audience spent (and I do mean spent) a whole day at Walt Disney World. This reminds me of a comment bouncing around the Internet: "Disney World is a people trap invented by a mouse." (As a side note: I really enjoy myself at Disney theme parks, so my comments are only intended as gentle humor.)

Secret 13: The Power-3 (context, structure, imposition)

The successful use of humor is about using effective patterns. Let's continue with the example "There's nothing free at Disney." *Context:* People spend money all day at Disney theme parks. *Structure:* The last word makes the joke funny. *Imposition:* The audience has feelings about being imposed upon by the pricing of Disney related items.

Secret 14: Twist a familiar phrase

Change a word and you make something funny. "Eat, drink and be merry, for tomorrow we economize." The original phrase is "Eat, drink and be merry, for tomorrow we die."

Secret 15: Set up the last word to have punch

Notice the last word in this example: "Take my wife—please!"

Secret 16: Go on a riff

A riff is a musical solo or a spontaneous improvisation. Here is an example: I was walking through Universal Studios, Florida, when I heard a rock and roll version of a classic Christmas song, "Oh, Holy Night." As my friend Sarah and I were listening to the song's phrase *Fall on your knees*, I said:

"That phrase Fall on your knees is one of the most powerful phrases in music—but not today.

"The melody is here; and the singer's somewhere over there.

"This is Sam's mother's favorite song. If she heard this version—she'd puke."

Let's notice that I went up the scale of intensity. I finished with an extreme word—puke.

Secret 17: Use the Magic of Three

In the above example we see the humor is structured in a pattern of three. The first statement sets up the situation. The second statement continues it. And the third statement twists the situation into a surprising direction.

Secret 18: Use the magic of the reoccurring joke

I once made a good rapport with a participant at a seminar. Because Joe demonstrated a good sense of humor, I made him the focus of some comments. He asked about the 15 judgments, a person makes about another person—which I call the four second barrier. I replied, "Someone meets you and thinks: nice suit, nice tie, needs Rogaine." Through the rest of the evening the comment about Joe's bald head became a reoccurring joke. Later I said, "What are the five forms of humor?" Joe replied, "Vicious"—and got a big laugh. I bowed Joe's way and said, "Forgive me."

Secret 19: Carefully use cynical humor

In the waiting area of the thrill ride Terminator 2: 3D at Universal Studios, Florida, TV monitors show mock commercials for the fictional company Cyberdyne (which, with no social conscience, created dangerous technology that destroys Terminator's world). The Cyberdyne commercial had a slogan: "We care so you don't have to."

Secret 20: Integrate current topics

One year, I witnessed the gruesome make-up show at Universal Studios. A goofy special-effects teacher discussed the then just-released remake of the movie *The Mummy*. He said, "The prince is sealed in a tomb of flesh-eating Pokemon." The audience laughed with glee.

Secret 21: Make fun of a safe target

While standing in line for the thrill ride Terminator 2: 3D at Universal Studios, my friend and I (and the crowd) became tired of waiting. An actress came out and played the role of the public relations person for Cyberdyne, the unfeeling corporation that created the humanity-crushing technology. The actress played the part well. Her character spoke in phony, ingratiating tones—and had a grating habit of saying, "Superrr." At one point she said, "No applause necessary." I said to my friend, "And none will be heard."

Secret 22: Put in an Act Out moment

An Act Out moment is when the humorist acts out his routine instead of just standing and telling the story. A comedian who Acts Out as another person will change his voice and posture to help the audience see the character. For example, if I was talking about a conceited CEO, I might perform (Act Out) his character. I would cross my arms, send my nose up into the air, and speak in a haughty tone. I would say: "I am a CEO. I know everything, I see everything, and I get indicted for everything."

Secret 23: Tie in the visual

At the Universal Studios gruesome make-up show, the goofy, special effects teacher pulled out a mannequin that looked like a shark had eaten half its body. He said, "This is Barbie. We have a special on Barbie today—half-off." The audience rocked with laughter.

When on vacation in the South of France, one of my friends heard another traveler commenting on vacationers' tendency to overeat. The traveler said, "If I eat any more I'll have to grease my legs to get my pants on."

Secret 24: Rehearse your choice of words before telling a story

Often a good story sounds better with concise words. Rehearse key phrases. Here is an example:

A man was getting tired of his wife always saying "Turn around, I think I left the iron on" when they were driving away, leaving for their annual trip. The next year, like clockwork, she waited until they were two miles away from home. She said, "Go back, I think I left the iron on." At a stoplight, the man pulled the iron from beneath his seat.

Notice how the story is told with few words.

Secret 25: Use similar sounds

One time on vacation, I turned to my loved one and said, "Ahh, what a sight to see: A flamingo doing the flamenco." She chuckled.

Secret 26: Use rhythm

Rhythm is a helpful component in humor. Here is an example expressed in the book, *The Healing Power of Humor*. Joan, a hospital nurse said, "I'm a body scratcher, patcher, wire attacher and bed pan snatcher."

Secret 27: Note goofy items from the newspaper

An essay contest in England entitled *Buy Britain* gave out prizes: radios made in Japan.

Secret 28: When speaking, use topic-oriented cartoons

When giving a presentation, it's easiest to warm up the room by projecting cartoons with a projector at the start of your talk. In this way, you don't have to worry about finding the right joke to set the tone of your presentation.

Secret 29: Use a label as you tell a story

I was coaching a client who wanted to make her story funnier. She mentioned a mean teacher at school who ate wasabe (the Japanese horseradish condiment). I suggested she label him *Wasabe-breath*.

Secret 30: Ad-lib in the moment

At a hospital, giving a presentation on *Say YES to Yourself: Successful Strategies for Conflict and Change in the Workplace*, I talked about working with a blunt, hard-charging director. In the moment, I improvised this comment: "Tell the bottom-line Director, 'The patients are still alive. It's a good day.'" The audience laughed.

Abundance is Built on Great Relationships

We warm up and deepen relationships with appropriate humor. Becoming skillful with expressing humor is worth every effort you make. For example, for years I shared a particular film clip to my students of my college course Science Fiction and Fantasy. The film clip was a scene from the feature film *The Abyss*, directed by James Cameron. The lead character "Bud," portrayed by Ed Harris, was introduced while he leads his team.

He gently, and with humor says, "Hey Harry. Do me a favor, will ya? Square away this mud hose, get rid of some of these empty sacks. This place is starting to look like my apartment."

Bud uses humor to guide his team members to keep the work area safe.

My students consistently said that they liked Bud. And this illustrates my point: appropriate humor warms up relationships.

With better relationships, you *wake up your spirit to prosperity*.

For example, this book was completed with editing work from some of my friends. One I have known and trusted for 26 years, and another for 29 years. And yes, we laugh together often.

Try experimenting with various forms of humor. Practice on safe audiences.

Here is a principle for your *Year of Awesome:*
Principle #8: Act to support friendships

Power Questions: How will you make space for relaxing times with friends? How will you encourage more laughter? Will you watch funny videos together, go to a comedy club, share funny anecdotes or something else?

September – Back to School

"Don't you want to learn?" Maria asked her little son Hector when he complained about going back to school.

Hector didn't mind learning; he dreaded being locked into his chair and following so many rules.

Instead, as adults, you and I can look upon learning as *our royal road to freedom!*

This relates to ….

Principle #9: Continue learning

What are we going to learn? How to **"Wake Up Your Spirit to Prosperity."**

In this section you will learn Seven Powerful Steps to create the life you really want, including an abundance of time and money, spiritual fulfillment and loving relationships.

Ever feel like you're in a financial rut? This section will shine the light on your natural brilliance. Your natural brilliance is like diamonds just waiting to sparkle when you shine a light on them. Your natural brilliance will light your way out of your financial rut.

The difficulties related to climbing out of a financial rut came up recently. My client Stephanie said, "I'm afraid that the higher I go, the further I have to fall."

"We'll find a way to bring your safety net up with you," I replied. I helped her explore alternatives and uncover her hidden talents. As an Executive Coach and Spoken Word Strategist, I help clients and audiences stretch and nurture their spirits during the process. I can do the same for you.

What makes this book different from others is that I combine both the spiritual and practical approaches to wealth. As a faculty instructor of Comparative Religion (for a duration of 14 years), I guide my college students to experience the beauty and power of spiritual paths.

I then provide business strategies from my roles as Executive Coach and "The Personal Branding Instructor" (as reported by *The San Francisco Examiner*). I guide my clients to take action to gain more money, do well in business, and expand feelings of fulfillment. You will learn secrets I have used and the strategies of 18 people—millionaires and billionaires.

This book incorporates spiritual and practical methods to increase wealth. As you learn these methods, you condition yourself to be at your best when it really counts.

In a later section, I will share with you the powerful process of Personaltainment™ Branding, a new level of branding I created.

Through this strategy my clients increase their customer base more quickly and also enjoy the process.

You can feel inner peace while you experience the ups and downs necessary to increase your personal wealth and fulfillment.

Further along, you will learn practical methods of the Momentum Action Plan™ (MAP), also known as the 9-Minute Miracle Breakthrough. Use this process once a week or at the beginning of your day to target and do the best actions to improve your life. Learn to add zest to your moment-to-moment experiences. You will also learn to use leverage, which is to gain the maximum benefits from the least efforts.

Later in this book, you will learn how to deepen and warm up your relationships because, as researchers have shown, quality relationships are the basis for great business success and personal fulfillment. You will also learn the *30 Secrets of Humor* to bring warmth and laughter to your relationships. Mark Burnett (creator of the TV shows *Survivor* and *The Apprentice* with Donald Trump) wrote, "Negotiation secret: If all else fails, make them laugh."

Enhancing relationships is a spiritual process. *Prosperity is about having more than money. It also includes financial freedom.*

Over the years my perspective has expanded as I enjoyed a number of adventures that required money, contacts and strategies. I am grateful for my experiences connected to prosperity including:

- Directing and producing feature films
- Traveling to various parts of the world
- Speaking at the National Association of Broadcasters Conference (the world's largest media conference) for six years in a row
- Teaching as a guest instructor at Stanford University
- Publishing my business books, music and novels
- Taking fun vacations with my romantic partner, her parents and my parents

From ordinary beginnings, I became the first college graduate in my family. I live with a lot of hope. In fact, a colleague asked me about my experiences of God; and I replied, "Times of delighted surprise."

Your path to enjoy more abundance begins now with this book. For more information concerning the topics in this book, you can reach me through my blog at YourBodySoulandProsperity.com

The central idea of *Wake Up Your Spirit to Prosperity* is to get out of your own way.

To manifest what you truly want, you need to change

your focus and wake up your spirit. Prosperity consciousness essentially means being awake.

Many of us experience great suffering concerning issues of money, prosperity and scarcity. Some don't realize that their financial details are part of their spiritual path. Spirituality includes the process of giving and receiving value. And prosperity is more than just money.

According to Dictionary.com, *prosperity* means "having success, flourishing, and having good fortune." It also states that prosperity is "an economic state of growth with rising profits and full employment." What we get from this definition is that prosperity is not just about money. Wake Up Your Spirit to Prosperity talks about spiritual growth and full employment of your natural brilliance, that is, your gifts from Higher Power.

For our discussion, we will use the process: S.P.I.R.I.T.

S – Seek the Higher View
P – Program for abundance
I – Intuit to do it
R – Retreat from Reverse-Examples
I – Inspire hope and faith
T – Target the good of all

In the following sections we will dive into the methods outlined with S.P.I.R.I.T.

You can turn your life into a positive adventure that includes abundance. This book shows you how.

Let's continue ...

Seek the Higher View

By emphasizing a Higher View, I invite you to make a transition to seeing things from the viewpoint of your Higher Self. You can focus on your Higher Self or remain stuck in the Ego. The Ego is made of fear. When you are stuck in your Ego you feel small, vulnerable and fragile. A number of people, when stuck in their Ego, feel irritable and angry. Anger is fear twisted.

On the other hand, you can focus on your Higher Self, or what I usually refer to as your True Self.

Your True Self is that part of you that is strong, focused and filled with natural brilliance and courage.

To get unstuck from your Ego and seek the Higher View is to make a transition to your Higher Self as fast as possible. When you're seeing things from your Higher Self, you experience a form of peace, even when things around you are chaotic.

In Taoism the idea is to flow with the universe. The Tao (translated as "The Way") is often compared to a stream of flowing water. Imagine how much more effective you would be if you were like a canoe flowing with the stream instead of like a rock, complaining about the water striking you in the face.

That is, avoid complaining about your stagnation and lack of opportunity. Flow with opportunities that appear.

How can you flow with the universe? How can you wake up your spirit? Focus on this question: How can I serve?

Your focus point is better when it goes beyond your personal needs. You need to see how to make a contribution. Martin Luther King, Jr. said, "Everyone can be great because anyone can serve." Where do you serve? Right where you are.

One of my clients said in desperation, "Serve? I can't serve. I'm barely keeping my head above water now." I shared with her that to *wake up her spirit to prosperity* is to expand her perceptions. Focusing only on one's urgent, immediate needs is like wearing blinders to the possibilities of service and, as a dividend, expanding earnings. The Ego is stuck in fear and is a small focus area.

To help you look beyond the Ego and its small focus area, let's view the differences between the Higher Self and the Ego.

Two Aspects of Your Self	
Higher Self	**Ego**
Abundance	Scarcity
Expansive	Contracting, pain-avoiding, reactive
Creative	Cowering
How may I serve?	What's in it for me?
Serve where you are.	Wait for a purpose to come along
Faith	Doubt
Love-mode	Fear-mode

The elements (above) related to the Higher Self all relate to Prosperity Consciousness.

On the other hand, all of the elements (above) related to the Ego relate to Scarcity Consciousness.

Back to Prosperity Consciousness: To attract prosperity focus on being in "love-mode." The idea of the love-mode is to focus on being helpful, which is a Higher Self approach. Also, many of us turn to Higher Power (some say "Spirit" or "God") who can guide us.

How do we, stuck in the real world and dealing with our daily lives, stay in the Higher Self? We memorize phrases that shift the directions of our thoughts.

Memorize phrases to shift your thoughts in a positive direction. Here are examples:
- Be still and know that I am God. (The Bible)
- Minds debate. Hearts relate. (Ann Wilson Schaef)

- We must not allow any force to make us feel like we don't count. Maintain a sense of dignity and respect. (Martin Luther King, Jr.)
- You must be the change you wish to see in the world. (Gandhi)
- Do not lay on any soul a load which you would not wish to be laid upon yours. (Baha'i)
- If you want others to be happy, practice compassion. If you want to be happy, practice compassion. (The Dalai Lama)
- You cannot solve a problem on the same level in which it was created. (Albert Einstein)
- Let no come to you without leaving better. (Mother Teresa)
- Our fears must never hold us back from pursuing our hopes. (John F. Kennedy)

Another way to shift your thoughts and feelings is through music. I can change my thoughts by humming the tune and words of an empowering song. And, I recall the exuberant music of *Indiana Jones* or *Superman, the Movie*.

Shifting your thoughts and feelings is important related to fear. We do not want get stuck in fear because that might prevent us from taking appropriate action. If you feel a touch of fear, realize that this is just a beginning. Now it's time to step forward.

Intensify the Power of Words

Some paragraphs ago, I shared a secret with you—the power of music. Our target is to use the power of your subconscious mind. In an article in *U.S. News and World Report*, writer Marianne Szegedy-Maszak reported: "Cognitive neuroscientists [identify that] most of our decisions, actions, emotions, and behavior depends on the 95 percent of brain activity that goes beyond our conscious awareness." Realizing this fact, I have my clients associate music, body posture, and an image to words they want to memorize.

For example, Phil played the theme music of *Superman, the Movie* while repeating the words from one of my books: "Courage is easier when I'm prepared." He stood up straight and strong as he held in mind an image of himself wearing a hero's cape. This combination of music, body posture, image and words helps Phil make decisions and take action when he is an empowered state of being.

I summarize this process with these words: *You must magnetize what you memorize.* Some magnets are empowered by a strong electrical current. Similarly, power-up your ability to shift to a Higher View by using a combination of words, music, body posture, and an image.

Principle: Shift to a Higher View. Shift the direction of your thoughts by using a combination of memorized phrases, music, body posture, and an image.

Author Tony Robbins said, "Successful people ask better questions, and as a result, they get better answers." Along these lines, I am including a Leverage Question for each of these sections. Leverage is like using a stick and a small rock as the fulcrum to move a boulder. Through leverage you can support the flow of grand abundance in your life.

Here is our first Leverage Question.

Leverage Question: What ideas do you want to memorize (and repeat to yourself) so you can quickly shift the direction of your thinking? What music, image and body posture can you add to engage your real power?

Program for Abundance

Another definition of prosperity is "a state of being very lively and profitable." It's your choice: You can live in love-mode or fear-mode. To achieve the best results, program your mind for abundance, which comes from the love-mode.

We seek to override the scarcity programming that may have been *placed there by parents or relatives.*

What does scarcity sound like? "We can't afford it." Abundance includes empowering phrases.

Mindsets	
Scarcity	**Abundance**
We can't afford it.	How can we gain more money?
	How can we serve more people?

Train your mind to see the abundance in life. Here's an example—A friend invites you to an event that is too costly. The idea is to reply with something that empowers you. You can say: "My family's budget is going in a different direction at the moment." Remember that your subconscious mind is listening at all times. Train it with thoughts of abundance, rather than thoughts of scarcity.

Budgets are a useful part of life. Budgets help people plan for vacations; and feature films get made via budgets. Learn to let go of your fear of that word. Do some research and find out the numbers before making a decision. For example, one of my clients, an aspiring author, discovered that she can self-publish copies of her book for only $75 (for a graphic designer for the book cover) through the print-on-demand process. She moved toward abundance and accomplished her goal of publishing, without getting bogged down in fear. The idea is to take a step forward.

For example, James Redfield first self-published his book *The Celestine Prophecy*. He sold the book from the trunk of his car. Then a major publisher took notice, and subsequently, over 20 million copies of Redfield's book were sold.

Find out the numbers, and you're one step closer to your dream.

It helps to drop "I can't afford it" from your speech pattern. "I can't afford it" puts you in a world of pain. Instead, put yourself into the world of possibility—a world of abundance.

One interviewer asked me: "The reality could be that someone really cannot afford it. What if the person really wants both things, and can only get one thing?" I responded by talking about a time, many years ago, when a friend and I were in a bookstore. I selected eight books but felt the need to put back seven. At the time my funds were needed for things like rent, food, and bus fare. But I wasn't disturbed because I knew that eventually I would have the money to get any book I wanted. However, my friend was upset. She didn't have the mindset that more prosperity was on the way.

One millionaire told me about a mindset that helped him. He had the phrase: "I'm a millionaire. The funds may not yet be in my bank account—but I'm a millionaire."

You need to program your thoughts and actions so that you support *the flow of abundance in your life.*

I encourage you to engage with the insights and methods throughout this book, particularly the questions at the end of each section. Becoming stronger is a process that requires you to take action.

When you are serious about opening the gate to a better flow of financial abundance, consider: A great idea is to make your work a prayer.

Mother Teresa said, "Prayer does not demand that we interrupt our work, but that we continue working as if it were a prayer."

To increase abundance, move beyond patterns that limit your progress, like trading your time for money.

When you want to make a leap beyond your current level of abundance, you need to get out of the limiting pattern of trading your time for money.

My next example comes from someone I have learned from directly, C.J. Hayden. Her book *Get Clients Now* details a methodology for effectively gaining clients in a way that fosters ease in her reader's life. To guarantee continued sales of her book, C.J. created the Licensee Kit, a program by which personal coaches use her book and methodology for their clients. To use C.J.'s successful program, coaches must ask their clients to buy copies of Get Clients Now. At the time of this writing the Complete Package, Training, and Renewable License is priced at $795.

From C.J.'s example, we learn to move beyond trading time for money. As a personal coach C.J. can only make an hourly fee. But the magic happened when she made the shift to being the creator of a franchise!

The Power-3 Income Streams

We can learn from C.J. Hayden about the process of creating multiple streams of income. But the crucial detail is to avoid scattering your energy. Several years ago, I learned this when a millionaire observed my business card and told me: "I see a lot of activity, but I don't know how productive it is."

I brought this insight into my executive coaching work. Over the years, I have seen clients who *dabbled in many money-making activities* before they met me. In response, I invited my clients to improve efficiency and reduce the number of scattered activities they were involved in. I introduced them to The Power-3 Income Streams:

- *Income Stream 1:* **Stability (your base).** One of my clients is a teacher, which forms her base. She can take appropriate time to analyze her stream of income opportunities. She is neither desperate nor harried.
- *Income Stream 2:* **Automatic.** A number of my clients make money through the Internet—while they are sleeping.
- *Income Stream 3: No ceiling.* A number of my clients are creating books, audio programs, and inventions. They know that when something becomes a hit, there is no ceiling on the amount of money they can make.

When creating a product, it is helpful to hear about the trials successful people endured. It often takes more than one product to become successful. For example, Richard Carlson, author of the *Don't Sweat the Small Stuff* series, told me that *Don't Sweat the Small Stuff* was his tenth book.

Another example: The ThighMaster® (promoted by Susanne Somers), which earned $100 million, was the second item on an eight-item plan of inventions. Peter Bieler, the leader of the ThighMaster team, knew that out of eight products some would fail and some would work. The team was fortunate: After the first item failed (and they learned from the process), the second item was a hit. Peter Bieler knew there was no ceiling to their future abundance.

Using the Power-3 Income Streams (Stability, Automatic and No Ceiling) helps you to avoid scattering your energy-and working on too many income streams at once.

Program for Abundance by Asking for Help

Another way to program for abundance is to ask for Higher Power's help. Best-selling authors Jack Canfield and Mark Victor Hansen (co-creators of the *Chicken Soup for the Soul* series) emphasize the power of asking. In their book *The Aladdin Factor* they describe hundreds of effective ways of asking for what you want.

Open the door to healing with the God Box

When you turn over your worries and cares to Higher Power, you open the door to healing. Write down what really troubles you and place it in a beautiful, small box—your God Box. Do not read the slip of paper ever again. As you place your paper in the box, recite a prayer like: "God, I turn this over to you. This is too big for me. I ask for Your help and healing so I feel better about this. I seek to do my part better. May this situation turn out for the good of all involved. Thank you. Amen."

Principle: Focus on abundance in every situation. Find ways to move beyond trading your time for money.

Leverage Question: How can I serve more effectively and keep abundance flowing?

[It helps to get a personal journal and answer the question posed at the end of each section. Take 20 seconds and write down your immediate thoughts. You'll gain more benefit from this process.]

Intuit to do it

When I talk about intuit to do it, I'm referring to a strategy that taps into your deepest powers. Intuit to do it means using your intuition to help gain energy, direction and the power to keep going until you complete something crucial to obtain abundance in your life.

"What if I'm intuition impaired?" asked a woman in one of my audiences.

"Perhaps, you're referring to the practice of not making space for your intuition," I responded. We all get feelings about things. We just need to acknowledge them and honor them. Dictionary.com defines *intuition* as "Immediate cognition ... The act or faculty of knowing or sensing without the use of rational processes ... An impression."

Sometimes we get a flash of insight or a gut feeling about something. For example, a woman seeking more customers for her barbershop realized she needed to reposition her business. She listened to her intuition which told her the best way to attract more male clients (her target customer) was to create a sports theme in her shop. She set up her barbershop like a sports bar with sporting events on the television set and sports-related magazines. Her business flourished, that is, prospered.

Researchers note that self-made millionaires follow through on their hunches. Also, a number of millionaires have said, "You only have to be right 51% of the time."

The important thing is to make space for your intuition.

I give speeches on the topic *Say YES to Yourself*. The idea is that you may need to say "no" to some things to create space so you can say "yes" to other things that focus on your top priorities.

I once gained 4 hours in 30 seconds. That is, I deleted four TV shows from my DVR (digital video recorder).

It's about making good choices. To make good choices we need to create *think-space*. When someone asks you to do something, give yourself time to think and, when it's appropriate, respond by saying: "I'll have to check my schedule when I get back to my desk. How about I call you this afternoon to see if I can fit that in?" This gives you the time and space to think about your decision to the offer.

So how do activate your intuition? First, think favorably about your intuition. Remember the times when you listened to your gut feelings and things turned out well. Second, make time for your intuition. Practitioners of Zen Buddhism and Hinduism set up time for daily meditation. Christians set time for daily prayer.

What if I don't have time for meditation?

One meditation guru was asked, "How long do you meditate?" He replied, "Three minutes a day." His point is that three minutes a day is better than planning to meditate 30 minutes a day—and you don't do it.

Will only three minutes do any good?

Yes. Zen Buddhists look for the sudden flash of insight known as satori, or intuitive illumination. A person can connect with Higher Power in just three minutes.

Carry a small memo pad in your pocket or purse so you can write down your insights. For example, some time ago I was riding a bicycle and, zap, I had an incredible idea for a novel or screenplay. This was a *Wow! idea*. I immediately wrote it down. (This idea became my book, *TimePulse: Beyond Titanic* ... free chapters visible at Amazon.com)

If you are driving it might be best to pull your car over to the side of the street. If you write slowly, you can carry an audio recorder. Just be sure to capture the idea. The universe has just handed you a gift. Honor the abundance of the universe and write it down.

Mozart captured musical ideas that flowed into his mind. He wrote in a letter: "When I am, as it were, completely myself, entirely alone, and of good cheer—say traveling in a carriage, or walking after a good meal, or during the night when I cannot sleep: it is on such occasions that my ideas flow best and most abundantly. Whence and how they come, I know not; nor can I force them. Those ideas that please me I keep in my memory [by humming] them to myself."

Make plans and take action because the universe bestows great ideas to many, but only a few have the courage and persistence to take action and make their dreams come true.

Make space for your intuition. Be ready when opportunities arise. For example, there have been times late at night when my sweetheart asks me about some future event. During late hours when I feel tired my reflex is to say "no." So I tell her the truth and say, "If I answer now, I'll say no. So instead, let's talk about this tomorrow, okay?" This is how I make space for my intuition and subconscious mind, which will ponder the event while I sleep.

Principle: Intuit to do it.

Leverage Question: How can you effectively and kindly respond to people and create *think-space* for yourself?

Retreat from Reverse Examples

Some negative people say "That's too much trouble." Or, "That will never work." We can look at negative people as

Reverse Examples. When you want a life of abundance and joy, you need to run—not walk—away from these people, the Reverse Examples.

I call negative people Reverse Examples because they are not standing still; they are actually going backwards. This is contrary to progress and does not support the flow of grand abundance.

I remember once walking to an appointment in downtown San Francisco. Two men were arguing loudly. In my mind I said a prayer: "Blessings to you both." These two men, through their abusive language and tone, were Reverse

Examples. They were not just standing still; they were causing damage to their relationship—and in effect they were going backwards.

When using the term Reverse Example to describe someone, it's important to realize that we are not judging that person, but defining a counterproductive action. No one has less value than any other person. The point here is that we need to value our intuition when selecting people to socialize with or think about. There are times when our intuition informs us that "I don't want to be like that person. She does not have the same goals I have. She doesn't want what I want. And she's not willing to pay the price I'm willing to pay to move forward."

Let's look at a healthy and spiritual way to interact with the people we call Reverse Examples. (Let's realize that a person can be both a good example in some area and a Reverse Example in another area.) People want closeness and competence. If you find yourself engaged in something that is creating space (a separation) and implying that the other person is not competent, STOP. Yes, stop. Even if you need to say, "Excuse me. I'll be right back. I need to go to the restroom."

When you return, identify something that you feel the other person is doing correctly. Also, identify your positive intention. For example, one evening, my sweetheart was watching television while I worked on a book—in another room. When I saw her after her programs, I felt uncomfortable. Instead of saying, "You're not spending enough time with me" which would put her on the defensive, I started with my intention and said gently: "I missed you." That created closeness.

When you want more abundance, watch out for the people who are focused on comfort first. These people don't take appropriate risks. Not taking appropriate risks can be a Reverse Example.

A Native American Elder (as quoted by Ann Wilson Schaef) said, "When the Creator gives you something, don't hesitate. Grab it." From this we realize that we must stretch to create a new phase of life that is different from all we have experienced thus far. To learn how to take appropriate risks, you need to feed your mind and spirit with examples of how people have accomplished the extraordinary. The process of successful and appropriate risk-taking is an important part of the journey to manifest wealth and a fulfilling life. And in this section, we will soon learn about risk-taking and more from selected Inspiring Examples: millionaires and billionaires.

The idea of retreat from Reverse Examples points to spiritual processes. People go on retreats to renew their spirits, minds and bodies. But you can have mini-retreats during your normal day. These are moments that align with Psalm 46:10: "Be still and know I am God." Some scholars point out that this means: Relax a moment and remember that God is running the universe.

A mini-retreat is a moment you take for yourself when you focus on a positive thought. When you do this you give yourself to Higher Power and offer up your stress. For example, when you walk to the restroom during a busy day at work, you can say a prayer in your mind—and have a mini-retreat.

The idea of "Be still and know I am God" and taking a mini retreat ties in with something called the Activity-Recovery Pattern. Researchers have found that the most effective people do not work fast and constantly and without breaks. The most productive people use an Activity-Recovery Pattern that includes times of rest and recovery.

For example, my morning often includes an intense period of writing. When I am done I get up from my computer or notepad and take time to exercise. My mind recovers while my body moves.

With my audiences, I emphasize *take breaks or be broken*. Pace yourself and use an Activity-Recovery Pattern.

Some people combine prayer and exercise. I know people who pray and walk on a treadmill for five minutes—three times a day for a daily total of 15 minutes. A landmark Harvard study noted that a mere 15 minutes a day for a total of one or two hours a week will improve a person's health. Those who do this have a 50% better chance to avoid a heart attack, and reduce the possibility of heart surgery. This is terrific news. In just 15 minutes you can combine exercise with prayer or meditation to achieve a healthy body and a healthy spirit.

People who procrastinate are Reverse Examples. On the other hand, people who enjoy abundance do not procrastinate. They take action. Here is a powerful tool I use every day: *The Morning 8*. Every morning for eight minutes I take action on whatever issue is crucial for my success. I find it helps to take on these challenges in the morning, when my mind and body are still fresh.

The Morning 8 is when you do what you don't like to do first thing in the morning, when your mind and body are fresh and free from the stress of the coming day.

For example, people who are buried in clutter might devote eight minutes each day to clearing their desks. Over a year (that is, 5 days a week for 51 weeks), that would add up to 34 hours. Imagine how your life could be free of clutter when 34 hours or almost a full work-week was devoted to eliminating disorder.

Avoid Reverse Examples & Seek Out Inspiring Ones

Reverse Examples have quick, easy answers to many new situations: "Don't do it; you'll get hurt" or "The odds are against you getting what you want."

The important idea is to move away from Reverse Examples and their limited patterns of thought. Seek out Inspiring Examples, that is, those people who have done the extraordinary!

Let's learn from fourteen millionaires and four billionaires about their processes to create financial abundance:

1. **Oprah Winfrey:** "Though I'm grateful for the blessings of wealth, it hasn't changed who I am. My feet are still on the ground. I'm just wearing better shoes." She also said, "The key to realizing a dream is to focus not on success but on significance—and then even the small steps and little victories along your path will take on greater meaning …. For every one of us that succeeds, it's because there's somebody there to show you the way out. The light doesn't always necessarily have to be in your family; for me it was teachers and school …. My philosophy is that not only are you responsible for your life, but doing the best at this moment puts you in the best place for the next moment …. You get in life what you have the courage to ask for." She also said, "Always continue the climb. It is possible for you to do whatever you choose, if you first get to know who you are and are willing to work with a power that is greater than ourselves to do it."

2. **Bill Gates:** "I think it's fair to say that personal computers have become the most empowering tool we've ever created. They're tools of communication, they're tools of creativity, and they can be shaped by their user." He also said, "It's a lot easier to connect to the story of the one person or the five people …. I know [that] there's 3 million

kids every year dying of things that are completely preventable with the technology we have today." And he said, "Your most unhappy customers are your greatest source of learning."

3. **Richard Branson:** "You don't learn to walk by following rules. You learn by doing, and by falling over …. Business opportunities are like buses, there's always another one coming …. A business has to be involving, it has to be fun, and it has to exercise your creative instincts …. Do not be embarrassed by your failures, learn from them and start again …. One thing is certain in business. You and everyone around you will make mistakes …. I never get the accountants in before I start up a business. It's done on gut feeling…"

4. **Mark Victor Hansen** (co-creator of the *Chicken Soup for the Soul* series): "You control your future, your destiny. What you think about comes about. By recording your dreams and goals on paper, you set in motion the process of becoming the person you most want to be. Put your future in good hands—your own."

5. **Jack Canfield** (co-creator of the *Chicken Soup for the Soul* series): "My life purpose is to inspire and empower people to live their highest vision in a context of love and joy." He also said, "You only have control of three things in your life—the thoughts you think, the images you visualize and the actions you take [your behavior] …. You cannot improve your life, your relationships, your game or your performance without feedback …. Slow down and pay attention."

6. **Marty Rodriguez** (Century 21's top real estate agent): "Many people become our friends and like to hang around here …. Clients bring their friends …. One time my husband asked, 'Why do you do these things? You don't have to do

these things.' I said, 'That's what makes me different.'"

7. **Tony Robbins** (top motivational speaker and author): "A real decision is measured by the fact that you've taken a new action. If there's no action, you haven't truly decided." He also said, "One reason so few of us achieve what we truly want is that we never direct our focus; we never concentrate our power. Most people dabble their way through life, never deciding to master anything in particular." Also, "The only limit to your impact is your imagination and commitment."

8. **Liz Claiborne** (founder of Liz Claiborne, Inc. who directed the company's designers): "[When I started the company] the goal was to clothe the working American woman. I was working myself, I wanted to look good, and I didn't think you should have to spend a fortune to do it …. I'm a great believer in fit, in comfort, in color. And I listened to the customer. I went on the selling floor as a saleswoman, went into the fitting room, heard what they liked and didn't like."

9. **Brian Tracy** (author of numerous bestselling self-help books): "I've found that luck is quite predictable. If you want more luck, take more chances. Be more active. Show up more often." He also said, "Successful people are always looking for opportunities to help others. Unsuccessful people are always asking, 'What's in it for me?'" He said, "The more you seek security, the less of it you have. But the more you seek opportunity, the more likely it is that you will achieve the security that you desire." Also, "All successful men and women are big dreamers. They imagine what their future could be, ideal in every respect, and then they work every day toward their distant vision, that goal or purpose."

10. **Warren Buffett** (listed by *Forbes* magazine as one of the richest people in the world): "I only buy what I

understand." He also said, "It's better to hang out with people better than you. Pick out associates whose behavior is better than yours, and you'll drift in that direction."

11. **Suze Orman** (#1 *New York Times* best-selling author, known as "America's most trusted personal finance expert"): "People first, then money, then things ... To choose [to be] rich is to make every penny count, every dollar count, every financial choice count." Also, "In all realms of life it takes courage to stretch your limits, express your power, and fulfill your potential ... it's no different in the financial realm." She wrote, "Truth Creates Money, Lies Destroy it."

12. **Robert G. Allen** (best-selling author): "Don't let the opinions of the average man sway you. Dream, and he thinks you're crazy. Succeed, and he thinks you're lucky. Acquire wealth, and he thinks you're greedy. Pay no attention. He simply doesn't understand." He also said, "When you're doing what you love to do, the money comes naturally. Maybe not at first, but eventually ... if you stick with it. Do you think Bob Hope started out with a goal, 'I want to become a millionaire by making people laugh, then I'll retire to do what I want'? I doubt it. He just did what he did best. And the money came."

13. **T. Harv Eker** (best-selling author): "Rich people associate with positive, successful people. Poor people associate with negative or unsuccessful people."

14. **George Lucas:** "If you want to be successful ... perseverance is one of the key qualities. It's very important that you find something that you care about, that you have a deep passion for, because you're going to have to devote a lot of your life to it ... You're not going to get anywhere without working extremely hard ... years and years of very, very difficult struggle through the whole process of achieving anything ... The secret is not to give up hope. It's

very hard not to because if you're really doing something worthwhile I think you will be pushed to the brink of hopelessness before you come through the other side. You just have to hang in through that."

15. **Steven Spielberg:** "A good director knows when to say 'yes.' ... The public has an appetite for anything about imagination ... I've found some kind of new color that I never splashed against the canvas before .... I don't need to prove anything to anyone. I don't need to prove anything to myself. I just need to stay interested."

16. **Harvey Mackay** (bestselling author of *Swim with the Sharks without Being Eaten Alive*): "What I'll be doing a year from now [is] undoubtedly based on contacts I made today."

17. **Mary Kay Ash**, founder of Mary Kay Cosmetics (with $4 billion in annual sales): "When I meet someone, I imagine her wearing an invisible sign that says, 'Make me feel important! ... This is one of the most important lessons in dealing with people I have ever learned." Also, "I believe each of us has God-given talents within us waiting to be brought into fruition." She wrote, "It was not extensive market surveys or demographic studies that created the pink Cadillac [her way to motivate consultants to excel], just [my] pure and simple woman's intuition." She noted: "The desire for recognition is a powerful motivator. Anyone who has attended a Mary Kay Seminar knows we recognize our people's achievement with beautiful gifts and tons of verbal appreciation. Exciting prizes are significant symbols of esteem: I believe both words and things are important." Finally, she said at a Mary Kay Seminar: "Are you ready for the most exciting moment of your life?"

18. **Walt Disney:** "We are not trying to entertain the critics. I'll take my chances with the public." Also, "Disneyland is a work of love. We didn't go into Disneyland

just with the idea of making money." "Build the castle first [so the construction crew knows the magic we're making]." He said, "You don't work for a dollar—you work to create and have fun." He noted, "Everyone has been remarkably influenced by a book." Also, "If we didn't have deadlines, we'd stagnate ... [To juggle so many things,] I'm always close to projects when we're chewing over the basic idea. Once the pattern is set ... I let the staff take over, and I go on to other things .... I have always had men working for me whose skills were greater than my own. I am an idea man .... Courage is the main quality of leadership ... usually it implies some risk—especially in new undertakings ... It is good to have a failure while you're young because it teaches you so much ... it makes you aware that such a thing can happen to anybody, and once you've lived through the worst, you're never quite as vulnerable afterward." Walt concluded, "I hope to stay young enough in spirit to never fear failure."

Wow! There are many useful strategies and wisdom condensed in what you have just read.

By the way, my life purpose is: *I help people experience enthusiasm, love and wisdom to fulfill big dreams.* And I am grateful to be working with you. Here is an important point: You can listen to the wisdom of millionaires and billionaires then go out and make new and powerful connections. In the next section we will see how I pulled together wisdom from effective people as I formulated Personaltainment™ Branding.

Principle: Retreat from Reverse Examples. Pay attention to what you need to learn and where you want to be.

Leverage Questions: Who and what are the Reverse Examples in your life? How can you get away from them or reduce your exposure time to them? Which people (who have already achieved what you want to do) can you focus on as Inspiring Examples? How can you use an Activity-Recovery Pattern?

Personaltainment Branding
Your Spiritual Path to Wealth

As I mentioned in the previous section, you can listen to the wisdom of millionaires and billionaires to learn to make new and powerful connections. That's how I formulated Personaltainment™ Branding. Personaltainment Branding can help you do well on the job—in a job interview, sales presentation or in building your own business.

Through Personaltainment Branding, I help my clients gain customers faster—with ease and feelings of personal fulfillment.

Personaltainment Branding is connecting with your prospective customers so they will know you and trust you quickly—and purchase what you offer.

For those of you who do not have external customers, you can still benefit from using the techniques in this chapter. Use these techniques with your supervisor and co-workers, who function like your internal customers. You still need to provide services for them, and you still need to keep them happy.

Let's continue to discuss branding. The standard form of branding is the association of a brand with an idea, like Volvo and safety. Similarly, Disney is associated with family entertainment—and theme parks.

Then there is personal branding (which we will cover in more depth in a later section of this book). Here is an example of a personal brand: Tom Marcoux, Executive

Coach and Spoken Word Strategist.

The central idea of a personal brand is to answer the question "What are you best known for?" For example, I use the phrase *"Take Command, Focus Your Brand"* which shows that I help people communicate powerfully through their brand.

I have designed Personaltainment Branding as a step up from personal branding. That is, when you use Personaltainment Branding, you have an advantage over conventional personal branding. The central idea of Personaltainment Branding is for you to create for your prospective customer an experience that is:

- Personalized
- Entertaining
- Connecting

I call this the PEC Triangle. Now I'll give you a specific example about "connecting."

My client Dr. JoAnn Dahlkoetter (bestselling author of *Your Performing Edge* at DrJoAnn.com) asked for my help on a press release during the 2006 Winter Olympic Games. As a coach to Olympic athletes, she wanted to be interviewed on numerous television and radio shows.

My first thought was that she needed to make her message connecting to ordinary viewers of TV and radio shows. The problem is that her clients, Olympians, are extraordinary people. How could she reach viewers? We decided to focus on what all people need: Skills to bounce back after a difficult struggle. I suggested that her press release include the following: "People must become skilled at bouncing back, whether it's crashing on ski slopes or crashing in a boardroom presentation," says Dr. JoAnn.

This was especially relevant because Dr. JoAnn had recently coached one of her Olympians to bounce back and regain confidence after a skiing accident that resulted in a concussion.

Finally, Dr. JoAnn's press release included this phrase:

"After Michelle Kwan's withdrawal and Jacobellis' fall, Dr. JoAnn Dahlkoetter can explain how people overcome fear and the strategies to recover quickly from failure."

Dr. JoAnn's press release secured interviews for her on NBC Television, Newsweek on Air/Associated Press Radio, KCBS Radio, Bloomberg on the Air in New York and many others.

You Can Use Personaltainment Branding at Work

These techniques only require a pen and sheet of paper—and the following effective questions.

Five Personaltainment Branding Questions
1. What about this is working for you? (personalized)
2. When did this become fun for you? (entertaining)
3. What's most important about this for you? (personalized)
4. In order for you to know that you have what you want, what has to happen? (connecting)
5. How can we make this work better for you? (connecting)

(Another version of Question 2 is: When could this become fun for you?)

You can use these questions with co-workers, prospective customers and current customers.

How Is Personaltainment Branding Spiritual?

In this book we talk about *how may I serve?* Also, we note that Mother Teresa said, "Make your work a prayer." Many of us seek to find spiritual and uplifting ways to work. Fortunately, the Personaltainment Branding process serves

the prospective customer in the following ways:
- Personalized means you are important to me.
- Entertaining is giving the customer an enjoyable experience.
- Connecting helps fill the customer's empty feeling of loneliness.

The Foundation of Personaltainment™ Branding

Now that you've had a taste of the process, let me describe how Personaltainment Branding first occurred to me. I listened to certain ideas from Bill Gates: "I think it's fair to say that personal computers have become the most empowering tool we've ever created. They're tools of communication, they're tools of creativity, and they can be shaped by their user."

I then recalled Tony Robbins' idea: "We aren't in an information age; we are in an entertainment age." Also, from Johnny Carson: "People will pay more to be entertained than to be educated."

I noticed the difference between Baskin-Robbins ice cream shops and Cold Stone Creamery. Baskin-Robins provides a selection of 31 Flavors. On the other hand, Cold Stone Creamery sells ice cream and the choice of add-ins, like chocolate syrup or fudge brownies. Cold Stone Creamery also provides helpful suggestions about add-ins that go together. One combination is called Cherry Cake Double Take®. The Cold Stone Creamery process is thus personalized.

With the iPod and iTunes, music is personalized. At the time of this writing, the online iTunes Music Store has sold more than 25 billion copies of songs.

You can make a lot of money by providing your service in a way that allows the customer to *personalize how he or she* uses the service.

We do best to move forward and let go of dinosaur thinking. Stubborn individuals who refuse to do so will become as extinct as the dinosaur! Look for ways to get ahead of the curve. Keep current by perusing the Internet (including blogs) to see what is in the global consciousness.

Now is the time of Personaltainment™—the time when prospective customers respond best to gestures that are personalized, entertaining and connecting.

Now we'll look at how Amazon.com customers have experiences that match the Personaltainment Branding process.

Example 1: A quick analysis of Amazon.com:

Personalized: Customers are given personalized recommendations based on past purchases and items placed in personal wish lists.

Entertaining: The customer's curiosity and feelings related to suspense are aroused so that she or he returns regularly to see what new items are being recommended.

Connecting: The customer can see lists like Listmania and So You Want To … that are written by other customers who share an interest. This might include advice, books and DVDs to help someone do something like write a book. This strategy develops the feeling of community.

Example 2: A quick analysis of Nightingale-Conant.com (a website for personal development):

Personalized: The prospective customer (or prospect) types answers about personal characteristics, into a form and gets a computer-designed Personal Mission Statement.

Entertaining: Receiving the Personal Mission Statement is fun, like seeing a daily horoscope at MSN.com.

Connecting: Having received something (the Personal

Mission Statement), the prospect feels a connection to Nightingale-Conant. The prospect will then browse the site to find educational programs that can assist in the realization of her or his dream.

Increase Your Abundance Using Personaltainment Branding

I created a form (visible in the next pages) to help a business owner or salesperson design a prospective customer's experience. With Personaltainment Branding, the idea is to make them go "Wow!"

Personaltainment™ Branding
Make them go "Wow!"

Example of website strategies

1. Personalized

See: Include a questionnaire to find out what energizes the prospective customer about his or her work.

Hear: Not applicable.

Touch: The prospective customer types in his or her responses to the questionnaire.

2. Entertaining

See: Prospect receives the computerized response to the questionnaire—which is like getting a horoscope: ("Oh, look at what it says!")

Hear: Include an audio link of the business owner praising the prospect for filling out the questionnaire. Music is played in the background.

Touch: The prospective customer types in her or his responses to questionnaire.

3. Connecting

See: Set up the questionnaire's response to include the prospect's first name in different places.

Hear: Include an audio link with the business owner saying: "Congratulations on devoting the time to fill out the form and get answers. We have found that highly motivated and effective people like you are the ones who complete the form and participate in the process. Well done. Now we will …"

Touch: Use music. Some music actually gives people a physical, positive response—a tingle along the spine, for example.

* * * * * *

Personaltainment Branding
Make them go "Wow!"

Website strategies

1. Personalized
See:
Hear:
Touch:

2. Entertaining
See:
Hear:
Touch:

3. Connecting
See:
Hear:
Touch:

(c) Tom Marcoux YourBodySoulandProsperity.com

Personaltainment Branding Does Not Require a Fancy Website ...

When you use the Five Personaltainment Branding Questions, you can devise a compelling experience for the prospective customer in any way you interact with the person—in-person, via email, and on the telephone. Again, here are the questions.

Five Personaltainment Branding Questions
1. What about this is working for you? (personalized)
2. When did this become fun for you? (entertaining)
3. What's most important about this for you? (personalized)
4. In order for you to know that you have what you want, what has to happen? (connecting)
5. How can we make this work better for you? (connecting)

For example, you are connecting when you ask someone, "What's most important to you about this?" The response you receive will give a clue as to how you can personalize your next comment and what you can offer that person.

Here's your opportunity to fill in a blank form to apply these ideas to your own work or service to customers. Personaltainment Branding is a helpful way to distinguish yourself in the marketplace. It is a powerful tool to give the prospective customer a Wow! experience that leads to becoming your customer faster. Personaltainment Branding also builds trust quickly. Everyone wins!

Furthermore, Personaltainment Branding is part of your spiritual path to wealth. It helps you wake up your spirit to prosperity. It helps you see things in a new light. It will give you a new perspective on how to serve people in the way they prefer to be served: personalized, entertaining and connecting.

Principle: To serve effectively, give the customer a Personaltainment Branding experience that is personalized, entertaining and connecting.

Leverage Question: Review the Personaltainment Branding process. How can you apply it to your work and use it to inspire prospective customers?

Inspire Hope and Faith

To experience a Higher-Self-mode of living, it is important to focus on hope and faith. Rabbi Harold Kushner wrote a book called *When All You've Ever Wanted Isn't Enough*. That's a powerful title. The truth is that many times what we thought we wanted is truly not enough. For example, a huge amount of money is not enough to bring inner peace. Johnny Carson said, "The only thing money gives you is the freedom of not worrying about money."

Hope and faith bring inner peace

At Dictionary.com, faith is defined as "a confident belief in the truth, value, or trustworthiness of a person, idea, or thing" and "a set of principles or beliefs."

So what do you believe? When you want more abundance, consider these beliefs:
- I learn from all experiences.
- Higher Power has a plan for me. Higher Power is watching over me.
- I am safe.
- I am worthy.
- Money is a tool I use well for the benefit of all.
- I easily gain money because I lovingly serve others in effective ways that attract money.
- To those God has given much, God enjoys their

enjoyment.

This last comment, "God enjoys their enjoyment," relates to Psalm 118:24: "This is the day the Lord has made; let us rejoice and be glad in it." It is appropriate and honorable to be grateful and rejoice. And rejoice means to feel happiness or joy—and to express great joy.

To express appreciation and joy is respectful of Higher Power. Be a fountain of positive energy, and your energy will bless the people around you.

Note that suffering is not the only road to wisdom. Misery not only loves company; misery creates company.

When you are feeling down, you can use a process to switch the direction of your thoughts: Take out a piece of paper (or just think this through in your mind) and write "I am grateful for ..." Then complete the sentence with ten examples. Instantly, your perception is expanded.

In my Comparative Religion college classes, I talk about healthy humility.

Healthy humility is acknowledging that *our ego often clouds our perception,* and we often do not know what supports our highest good.

Since we often do not know what supports our highest good, an effective prayer includes an ending of "this situation or better." My client Sandra wants a particular agent to represent her books, but then she remembers to add to her prayer: "this agent or an agent that would be a better match for me and my material."

We need to be humble. We don't see the whole picture in a given moment. Author Tama J. Kieves wrote: "The path of inspiration defies navigation. We arrive by way of revelation."

We live in hope and faith. And we live to witness revelations in our lives. Our search for personal truth goes like this: We receive a bit of guidance. We climb to a peak. We see more. Then we start up to a higher peak.

Joe Karbo, author of *The Lazy Man's Way to Riches*, took such a journey. Joe was deeply in debt. He consulted four lawyers and a judge and learned the extent of the law and how to interact with creditors to gain agreement to reasonable payment plans. He wrote a book based on his experiences that sold 100,000 copies, which significantly reduced his debt.

To create abundance, many people learn to solve a problem—and then teach others how to solve that problem.

To increase abundance, focus on hope. Mary Kay Ash, founder of Mary Kay Cosmetics (with $2 billion in annual sales), said, "Give yourself something to work toward—constantly." Write down what you are looking forward to. For example, one goal can be to earn extra money for a family vacation.

Also, when you design a product or service, have it serve people's hopes. Author Peter Nivio Zarlenga said, "In our factory, we make lipstick. In our advertising, we sell hope."

The important point to remember is that we can choose beliefs that support our path of abundance. We can believe that we have natural abilities and that Higher Power will help us to serve many people, and as a dividend, earn financial freedom.

Principle: Choose beliefs that build up your spirit and personal energy.

Leverage Question: Which of your beliefs support your path toward abundance?

Target the Good of All

One definition of prosperity is tending to favor or bring good luck. When you target the good for all involved, you align with the goodness of the universe. And this helps you attract good luck.

Let's begin by talking about forgiveness. In his book *Forgive For Good*, Dr. Fred Luskin talks about forgiveness as the process by which one ends a personal cycle of blame and suffering. We learn to become the hero of our own story instead of being a victim. One of my clients said, "My brother always beat me up when I was young." Imagine the power that emerges with the following substitution: "This is when I learned to value protecting myself. I asked my parents for karate lessons."

Consider this belief:

I can use everything to help me grow and serve more effectively.

When you focus on this belief, you can support a grand flow of abundance in your life. Learn to forgive—to free up your energy and create more abundance.

This section is about targeting the good of all. By all, I mean include yourself, your family, friends and your Higher Power.

Targeting the good of all is really about forgiveness, which is defined here as "seeing the big picture." The big picture is a more helpful definition of the word *forgiveness* than its more traditional meaning—*pardon*, a word that locks us into seeing a guilty person only as one who avoids punishment.

On the other hand, viewing forgiveness as the big picture allows us to go through the process of letting go of our painful feelings. For example, my client Marina received a huge disappointment. For months she helped her friend Janet organize a conference. Marina assumed she would be rewarded with an opportunity to give a presentation at the event. Marina's speaking business was just starting, and she really needed a break. Marina had expressed to Janet her desire to give a speech.

At the last minute Marina discovered that she was not included on the conference agenda. It broke her heart. How could her friend Janet be so unfair and cruel?

I guided Marina through the Big Picture Forgiveness Process. Using the four-step process, Marina began by acknowledging her personal truth, which was that she felt deeply hurt. She overcame her disappointment by expanding her perspective.

The Big Picture Forgiveness Process

Step One: Acknowledge the pain. Marina said, "I'm really disappointed and hurt that Janet didn't give me the opportunity to serve her audience—especially after the help I gave her with the conference preparation."

Step Two: Take care of yourself. Marina treated herself with warm baths, relaxing music and time to write in her journal. She also processed her feelings as we talked through the situation.

Step Three: Examine the situation from the perspective of a metaphorical helicopter—to gain objectivity. In time, Marina was able to say, "Janet didn't include me on her list because she was only including speakers who already had a long list of fans. Janet was only focused on making her conference a success. I can understand that. But I still feel that she could have included me in some way. Since it was a spiritual conference, perhaps I could have led the prayer at dinner time."

Step Four: Become the hero of your own story. Marina eventually said, "When Janet didn't include me in the conference, it became a warning sign that I need to change my perspective. I need to have faith that God will provide me with other opportunities. Also, I need to step up my participation. I need to intensify my focus. I really want to devote more time to marketing my own speaking career. I can't control what others do, but I can make better choices for myself."

Months later Marina still talks to Janet on the telephone from time to time. Marina's healthy approach to forgiveness has saved a friendship—and perhaps opened the door for her friendship with Janet to deepen over time. The good news is Marina is now free of her painful feelings. Her time and energy have been set free, too.

Within the word "forgiveness" are the letters that spell the word "free."

The Good of All Means Everyone Profits from a Situation

We start enjoying life to the fullest when we have learned to let go of hesitation around the word *profit*. Dictionary.com defines profit as "an advantageous gain or return; benefit." When you put service and Higher Power first, you can create profit in a holistic manner.

Author Harold Kushner wrote: "Our souls are not hungry for fame, comfort, wealth, or power ... Our souls are hungry for meaning."

To unlock the floodgates of abundance, we use this question:

How can you expand how you serve, in ways that are profitable and result in the dividend of abundance?

One speaker said, "Marriage is a place where you go to give—not just go to get." Find out how you can expand your contribution to the people in your life. And don't be shy about looking for profitable ways to accomplish your goals. For example, years ago, when working in a retail environment, I was trained to ask, "So what brings you into the store today?" I learned to say it in a friendly way.

However, I would not be encouraging the customer to buy something if I approached her by only saying "How are you today?" I would not be serving both the person and the store.

You can make the interaction profitable for the person and for the store.

To target the good of all is to focus on how we conduct our daily lives. When I was in Japan, I witnessed a festival (known as matsuri) that is part of the indigenous religion Shinto. Shinto includes affirmations for family, tradition, reverence toward nature, physical cleanliness and festivals. The idea is, you can uplift your life when you affirm the valuable parts of it. Festivals, celebrations and rituals of worship that honor the Divine are helpful.

Author Sue Patton Thoele wrote: "Soothe your soul with ritual." Rituals keep spirituality in mind. Rituals remind people they are in a relationship with the Divine, and that relationship requires effort and time.

My client Mary celebrates her gratitude for her writing talent with a ritual, her annual "Joy in Writing Day." She purchases a book (she loves books), and she writes something for fun.

Rituals can be simple, brief and meaningful:

At every meal my sweetheart and I hold hands and say together, "We're grateful. Thank you."

Principle: Target the good of all involved.

Leverage Question: How can you expand how you serve, in ways that are profitable and result in the dividend of abundance?

* * *

We have discussed the process S.P.I.R.I.T. and have examined the principles and Leverage Questions that will inspire you to achieve and support a grand flow of abundance in your life.

S – Seek the Higher View
P – Program for abundance
I – Intuit to do it
R – Retreat from Reverse Examples
I – Inspire hope and faith
T – Target the good of all

I have presented Seven Secrets (to wake up your spirit to prosperity), that include:

- The six methods of S.P.I.R.I.T., plus …
- The process to serve the customer effectively: a Personaltainment™ Branding experience that is personalized, entertaining and connecting.

Author David Kundtz wrote that "Spirituality is the meanings and values by which you live your life combined with, for believers, the way your experience the divine. The combination of God, meanings and values is spirituality."

Walt Disney's brother and partner, Roy O. Disney, said, "Decision-making is easy if your values are clear."

You have the power to choose your beliefs and choose how you live on a daily basis. You can choose to focus on scarcity or abundance. You can remind yourself with "I am grateful for …"

As I mentioned earlier, before I go to sleep each night I write in my Daily Journal of Victories and Blessings. A victory relates to an action I took—like exercising. A blessing is a gift—like talking on the telephone with an extended family member. I go to sleep feeling grateful for the blessings and adventures of each day.

I am grateful for the opportunity to connect with you through this book. I wish you a journey of love, abundance and blessings.

Here is a principle for your *Year of Awesome:*
Principle #9: Continue learning

Power Questions: How will you learn something new every day? Will you listen to audio programs or read a page every morning? Will you watch educational videos or attend workshops?

October – Halloween

A number of reports suggest that modern practices of Halloween grew out of the ancient Celtic festival of Samhain. Festival participants would light bonfires and wear costumes to ward off roaming spirits.

We may wear costumes on Halloween, but we also wear "masks" every day. We assume roles. The problem is that we may have outgrown a role (mask) but stepping forward feels like stepping off a cliff into the unknown.

The powerful plan is to take small actions in the positive direction of more and better in your life.

This relates to …

Principle #10: Target "act it until you become it."

In recent years, there has been some controversy over the recent feature film portrayal of Superman. (Yes, a comic book character; we are talking about Halloween.) A number of people describe the new cinematic version of Superman (portrayed by Henry Cavill, under the direction of Zack Snyder) as a "mopey guy."

On the other hand, the 1978 Superman (portrayed by Christopher Reeve) was friendly guy, happy to help out.

In fact, when Lois Lane asked, "Who are you?"—Superman replied, "A friend."

In the recent feature film, *Batman v. Superman: Dawn of Justice,* Superman's earth mother says, "Be their hero, Clark. Be their angel, be their monument, be anything they need you to be... or be none of it. You don't owe this world a thing."

That's not the point!

In 1978, Superman acted in a kind, friendly manner because that was *his way of being in the world.*

My point here is: Act it Until You Become It is about you choosing **how you want to be in the world**.

It's *not* about winning anyone's approval.

It's about expressing the creativity and joy that's deep in your True Self.

This idea of Act It Until You Become It is based on philosophy and science.

"Actions seems to follow feeling, but really actions and feeling go together; and by regulating the action, which is under the more direct control of the will, we can indirectly regulate the feeling, which is not. Thus the sovereign voluntary path to cheerfulness, if our cheerfulness be lost, is to sit up cheerfully and to act and speak as if cheerfulness were already there." – William James

"It is easier to act yourself into a new way of feeling than to feel yourself into a new way of acting." – Harry Stack Sullivan

So do you want to feel like a confident person? Act It Until You Become It. Stand like a confident person. Move like a confident person.

I've actually guided clients to imagine how they would stand with a Superman (or Supergirl) cape on their shoulders. Boom!—better posture. A smile on the face.

Here is a principle for your *Year of Awesome*:
Principle #10: Act It Until You Become It

Power Question: How do you really want to "be in the world"? Do you want to express strength, resolve, courage, kindness and creativity? Act It Until You Become It!

November – Thanksgiving

At the dinner table, with friends and family, I guided everyone to take each person's hands and say together, "We're grateful."

The idea of gratitude transcends spiritual paths, and atheists I know have found value in gratitude, too.

Principle #11: Nurture gratitude.

"If the only prayer you ever say in your entire life is thank you, it will be enough." – Meister Eckhart

Shifting your thoughts to gratitude blesses you and everyone near you. Why? Because when you shift to gratitude you guide yourself away from fear and thoughts of lack and scarcity.

By definition, when you're grateful about something, you *have* the something!

One of my mentors pointed out that we can *also* be grateful for the absence of something—for example, the absence of the pain of a temporary illness.

Every day, I write down "I'm grateful" next to my notation of using a sinus rinse. In the years of using a sinus rinse, I have enjoyed greater health. I'm grateful!

Here is a principle for your *Year of Awesome:*
Principle #11: Nurture gratitude.

Power Question: How will you consciously choose more times of feeling grateful? (You could recite to yourself a list of "10 Blessings" while you take a shower. That is, you identify things you're grateful for. In this way you clean your body and mind. You experience renewal.)

December – Holiday Season

The word "holiday" is derived from the Old English word hāligdæg (hālig "holy" + dæg "day"). We're talking about a holy day.

What's holy to you?

Or in other words …

What's sacred to you?

What's most important to you?

This relates to …

Principle #12: Open with "the sacred"

When I say "open with" I mean, *make it first*. Literally. I often begin my day with writing. No emails. Not even breakfast. Why? As I wake up, my subconscious mind is fresh and renewed after a night of sleep.

One of my clients begins each day with 8 minutes of clearing clutter. Why? She wants her apartment to be a place of rest and renewal, and she has discovered that being "buried in clutter" is sapping her precious energy.

Here is a principle for your *Year of Awesome*:
Principle #12: Open with "the sacred"

Power Questions: What is sacred to you? How will you start your day? (With reading something inspirational? With writing? Taking a walk. Hugging your spouse? Singing? Meditation? Prayer? Or something else …?)

BONUS Principle: Win by Listening

When it comes to S.U.C.C.E.S.S.A.C.T.N.O.W., the final letter is W for *Win by listening.*

I emphasize with my clients and college students: **When you're listening, you're winning.**

A number of misguided men have remained in the role of "Mr. Fix-It." They offer advice or prescriptions when simply listening would be the action that develops harmony and closeness.

I've learned to ask, with friends, "Would you like me to brainstorm with you about that or would you like me to just listen?" Often, a friend picks "listen to me."

Why? Because having a good listener in your life can be rare!

Improve your relationships; learn to listen more.

By the way, during the Holiday Season, we give gifts. What's a great gift? Offer friends and family your compassionate, heartfelt listening.

Book Two:
10 Seconds to Wealth – Additional Topics

What does it take to create more prosperity in your life? Being at your best during the crucial moments in your daily life. Learn to make another person comfortable. If you accomplish that, you'll be able to often secure his or her cooperation and build a prosperous future with mutual benefits.

We'll explore these topics:
1) The Effective 10 Seconds When You Meet A New Person
2) The Effective 10 Seconds When You Close Your Speech And Ask for What You Want
3) The Effective 10 Seconds When You Really Listen and Make Someone Feel Important

1) The Effective 10 Seconds When You Meet A New Person

When you meet someone for the first time, your goal is to set the person at ease. Begin with questions that are easy and fun for the person to answer.

You could begin with "Hi, I'm [your name]. And you are?"

Then, depending on the situation, you could ask a question similar to one of these:
- How do you know our host Mark?
- What presentation at this conference are you looking forward to?

I call such questions which are *easy and fun to answer* "Gentle Questions."

The above questions may not seem to be "fun" to answer. For fun, help the person talk about what he or she likes to talk about. One way to do that is ask, "What are you looking forward to?"

Usually, the person asks in return, "About what? A vacation? At work?"

You can reply: "Sure. Whichever one is more fun."

Become More Comfortable and You're Likely to Set a Person at Ease

The way to really help another person feel at ease is to "do your homework" so you are as comfortable as you can be. Your homework is to choose a number of questions and something you intend to say and then *rehearse* the things you want to discuss before the event.

For example, some years ago, I signed up for a workshop and made a plan to introduce myself to the workshop leader, a top person in industry.

Before the event, I rehearsed with friends. My plan was to walk up to the workshop leader and say, "Hello Frank, I'm Tom and we share something in common. We both went to Santa Clara University. I was wondering how your experience was as a board member of . . ."

For some of us, it is even a good idea to rehearse smiling. Instead of just practicing the placement of a "fake smile," I choose to think of something pleasant. I associate the pleasant thought with smiling.

For example, before meeting Frank, I told myself, "It's going to be fun for Frank to meet me. I'm going to listen to him a lot and he'll feel good."

Starting with a positive thought naturally shifts your internal state of being and causes your encounter with the individual to be more genuine. This in turn allows the person you are trying to connect with to feel more comfortable around you and establishes an initial point of trust. That's much better than trying to toss on a stiff, fake smile. The use of a positive thought fosters the beginning of a good relationship.

So for those crucial first 10 seconds of meeting someone you have three tools.
- a warm smile
- Gentle Questions
- your comfort developed through rehearsal

Rehearsal can help you quiet down nervous feelings. Will you get to some state of total comfort and confidence? For many of us, that's unlikely. As a trained actor, I learned to take nervous feelings and use them as energy for rehearsal and being "fully alive" during a performance.

Meeting someone for the first is not about pretending or faking it. But it does require energy. So I invite you to use your nervous feelings as a source of energy.

With my clients and college students, I give them an image and phrase to remember. Picture a kind grandmother saying: "Feeling fear? Rehearse, my dear."

The *10 Seconds to Wealth* blossoms when you set another person at ease and make him or her feel important.

That person will have a good time and he or she will be more likely to cooperate or even help you on your path of abundance and prosperity.

2) The Effective 10 Seconds When You Close Your Speech And Ask for What You Want

For years, I have coached clients and graduate students in how to close a speech, ask for funding or have their thesis project approved. I combined research studies with my own methods to provide a powerful way to close your speech.

Here is the format that I suggest:

You say, "Because of [Reason #1] and [Reason #2], I encourage you to please say 'yes' to my project."

The final words of your statement can be:
- Funding my project
- Reading my screenplay
- Greenlighting my feature film

3 Elements of *the Power Close to Your Speech*

I train my clients to use the 3 *Elements* so their final statement (before "Thank you") gets the cooperation they're asking for.

By the way, nothing "sells itself." YOU need to ask for the order (or sale). That is, you need to ask for what you want. Even if someone is poised to say "yes" to your product or service, they still need you *to invite* them to go ahead and buy your product or service. In fact, some people, on a subconscious level, need "permission" to buy. How do you grant that permission? You use the First Element:

Element #1: Provide "Because" and Two Good Reasons

The classic principle of selling is: People buy on emotion

and later justify on facts. When you refer to two good reasons, you are, in a sense giving people permission to buy because they have *good reasons* to purchase your product or service!

We also provide two reasons because you have two chances to land on the reason that moves the person to say, "Yes."

"Because" is an important part of the process. Why? Research showed that people will more often comply when hearing "Because."

In one study*, a person with papers cut ahead of other people in line waiting to use a copy machine. He simply said, "Excuse me, I have 5 pages. May I use the Xerox machine, *because* I have to make copies?"

The people in line allowed the person cut ahead. When the person did not say *because*, he was met with resistance.

Be sure to say "Because" to guide people to welcome your offer.

[*The study is referred to in the article: Langer, E., Blank, A., & Chanowitz, B. (1978). "The Mindlessness of Ostensibly Thoughtful Action: The Role of 'Placebic' Information in Interpersonal Interaction." While I earned a degree in psychology, I came across this classic study.]

Element #2: Put "Yes" into the Room

When I would go on auditions for film and television roles, I discovered the power of placing "yes" into the room. For example, one year I had auditioned for a commercial. Then, I said to the three people overseeing the auditions, "I hope you'll say *Yes* to my being in your commercial." I nodded a bit. The center person nodded in return and turned to the person on his left and asked, "Yes?" The person nodded. He then turned to the person on his right who replied, "Yeah."

The role in the commercial was mine!

Element #3: Use Words that Acknowledge the Person's Power

I've guided graduate students to say: "… I hope you'll please say yes to my thesis." In academia, committees hold great power and so the student is wise to acknowledge their power by using the words "I hope."

In business, we ask people to do things. We avoid appearing arrogant when we use words like "I encourage you"; "I invite you" and "please."

Here's a secret. When you say, "please," voice it in a gentle way. However, when you voice "say yes," use a confident tone. Why? *Please* confirms the other person's power, while *"say yes"* demonstrates that you are certain that your project *is* valuable.

Finally, be sure to rehearse in front of people your phrase "Because of [Reason #1] and [Reason #2]."

You want this phrase to come out easily and smoothly. Say it with confidence.

The end of your speech is a crucial part of *10 Seconds to Wealth*. Rehearse. Prove to yourself that you are ready to give a presentation and enjoy all the times you will hear "yes."

3) The Effective 10 Seconds When You Really Listen and Make Someone Feel Important

Want someone to feel important? Really *listen* to him or her. Unfortunately, many of us have zero training in how to listen. Worse yet, our brains tend to function at 700 words a minute with a lot of negative, "re-run" thoughts clogging our ability to listen in the present moment.

How do we become better at listening? We identify principles and we rehearse using simple methods to be present for the other person.

We'll use the N.O.W. process:

N – nix telling *your* story

O – open with gentle questions

W – wrangle your Reflective Replies

1. Nix telling *your* story

"Nix" is a way of saying "Stop that!" Many of us respond to something the other person says by replying, "Oh, yeah. That reminds me when I went through something like that…"

We think we're being supportive, but in reality we just took the spotlight off the person and we're now the "star" of the conversation and we're talking about *our story*. In effect, we've "hijacked" the conversation.

Stop that!

Instead, ask a gentle question to encourage the other person to keep talking.

You can ask questions like:

- That sounds intense. So what happened next?
- Oh. How did you feel about that?
- So how would you like things to go?

Pay close attention. If you find yourself talking about your past history, pause and ask a gentle question that encourages the person to keep talking.

2. Open with gentle questions

I've just mentioned the "gentle question." I've learned that crafting a *neutral* question really helps. For example, I often begin chatting with someone on Facebook or gmail, by asking the neutral "How are things going for you?"

Often people complain about something in their life. Then I reply with supportive comments like "That sounds intense" and "And then what happened?"

I've learned to be careful about certain questions. A couple of people I know do *not* like the question "What are you looking forward to?" Two people have told me that they feel like they're being quizzed and their response will be graded. Fortunately, the vast majority of people I interact with are not that intense or sensitive. [In person at a networking event, I still advocate using "What are you looking forward to?" as a question to get someone to talk about what they like."]

Sometimes, I ask, "So what's new?"

3. Wrangle your Reflective Replies

I coined the term *Reflective Reply* to mean a response you make that reflects or acknowledges the speaker's feelings.

Here are examples:
- That sounds intense.
- That sounds frustrating.
- That sounds like it felt good.

Saying "that sounds" is vital because you *avoid* telling someone how he or she feels. You give the person the chance to clarify the real feelings.

According to researchers, people want to be *heard* and to be *known*.

Imagine how in any romantic comedy, when one romantic partner does something nice. The feeling is: "You really know me. And you accept me and love me."

Remember, to make someone feel important, listen well to the person. Let's continue with the next section …

Book Three:
10 Seconds to Wealth – More Topics

Now we'll explore how to be at your best in various important situations from negotiating to improving your personal relationships.

We'll explore these topics:
1) The Effective 10 Seconds When You Negotiate for a Better Deal
2) The Effective 10 Seconds When You Work with Creditors
3) The Effective 10 Seconds When You Shift Yourself into an Empowered State of Being
4) The Effective 10 Seconds to Inspire Forgiveness When You Make a Mistake
5) The Effective 10 Seconds to Enhance Your Romantic Relationship

1) The Effective 10 Seconds When You Negotiate for a Better Deal

For the *10 Seconds to Wealth* to work well for you, be sure get yourself into a state of being in which you feel prepared. First, prepare two things: your Maximum Supportable Position (MSP) and Least Acceptable Result (LAR).

Your MSP is the high end of what you say that you want. It's not "crazy and unsupportable." It makes sense. You have a rationale for stating your comment. You might say something like: "I want $16,000 for this car. That's the value that the Blue Book says."

The LAR is the absolute minimum you'll accept for the car, for example. If you told yourself, "I'll accept $10,000 as the lowest amount" then anything you get over $10,000 is a deal in which "you are winning."

You'll feel stronger during a negotiation when you know the above two figures MSP and LAR. You'll know your own requirements.

Phrases to Use during the Crucial 10 Seconds

Pre-plan what you will say before you are in the negotiation situation. You can use phrases like:
- We'll need you to find a way to do better than that.
- So I'm sure I was clear: You know that this product has ___, ___ and ___ that can really help you at the office, right? So is $597, *the best* you can do?

I invite you to practice the above phrases. Rehearse in front of friends. Get your mouth used to saying such phrases.

Then in the *10 Seconds to Wealth*, you'll feel prepared and the negotiation is more likely to go your way.

2) The Effective 10 Seconds When You Work with Creditors

To be effective in the crucial 10 seconds when you are

working with a creditor, you need to prepare.

Here are **3 Elements of Working Well with a Creditor**

Element #1: Write your script and rehearse

One potential script is: "I want to start things going in a positive direction. How about I begin by sending $5.00 per month?"

The person on the phone will likely protest but do not give up. Use what is known as the "Broken Record" method. (Years ago, a vinyl record (disk) would get stuck and then a portion of the recording would repeat over and over.)

The "Broken Record" method includes a person repeating a certain idea or offer again and again.

You repeat your comment gently: "As I mentioned, I can begin with $5.00 per month."

When you rehearse and later have the written script in front of you, you'll do better.

Be sure to keep your tone pleasant. In fact, it often helps to say to the person on the phone, "Thanks for making this process as pleasant as possible."

In this way, you engender a positive interaction.

Element #2: Talk with the Right Person

Over the years, when working with a particular business (whether an Internet Service Provider or another company), I learned to sometimes say, "It looks like it's time for me to talk with your supervisor."

The right person has the power to help you.

Most clerks simply parrot back "the policy is..."

A manager can often say, "Okay. I can only do this thing one time and only for you . . ."

(Some clerks resist passing you to the manager. Ask, "Are you saying that I cannot talk with a manager?" At that point, since the clerk knows that the call is usually being recorded, he or she will reply, "Uh, I'm not saying you cannot talk with a manager." You respond, "Good! Then please pass me to your manager. Thank you.")

Element #3: You control when you need to end the conversation.

If things are going terribly, you can end the conversation. It is best if your write down and rehearse conversation enders like:
- Oh, someone just came in the room. I need to take care of something. I'll have to call another time. Thanks. Goodbye.
- Oh, something has just come up over here. I must go. Have a good day.

* * *

As we saw with the above material, the crucial 10 Seconds can be improved by both writing a script for what you want to say and then rehearsing it. It is important to use all the tools you have to help you improve your skills when it comes to negotiating exactly what you want from those who have the potential to give you what you want. Be sure to rehearse and to take action to improve.

3) The Effective 10 Seconds When You Shift Yourself into an Empowered State of Being

If you're feeling in a low mood, remember these three powerful words: "Breath and Gratitude."

"Belly Breathing" helps many people calm down even when confronted with a tough situation.

I know it works because from the ages of 9 through my teen years, I did deep breathing and closing my eyes at the beginning and ending of each karate class I attended.

This made a big difference when my father grabbed me yet again by the hair. An abuser, he would grab me by the hair and throw me into walls.

But I had just turned 15 years old and I had earned a second degree brown belt in karate.

I had to stop my father from assaulting me yet again. My karate training had me poised to punch him in the mouth.

But this was my father!

These were 10 crucial seconds of my life.

If I punched my father, his Marine training would likely kick in and the consequences could be a severe injury or accidental death to one of us.

The deep breathing I had practiced has conditioned me. I suddenly went calm, and I made a calm decision: I punched a hole in the wall. I did *not* strike my father.

"Goddammit, look what you did to the wall!" he yelled. But he never grabbed my hair again.

I'm not talking about theories here. I know that deep breathing can put you into an empowered state.

"Belly breathing" begins when you inhale deeply through your nose. Allow your abdomen to inflate. ("Let your belly get big.") Hold your breath for a moment. Then breathe out through your mouth.

Some people choose to count. However, I find it better to use words. My clients use empowering words like:
- I am relaxed.
- God relaxes me.
- I am love.

You can say your affirmation one time (in your mind) as you breathe in. You can repeat it as you hold your breath. And you can repeat it twice as you breathe out.

The other thing that can place you in an empowered

state is gratitude. I'm grateful that I had the calm to *not* strike my own father. And I still accomplished what I needed to do: I stopped the abuse.

The fastest way you can get to gratitude is to say out loud: "I am grateful for ____" and then say something that means a lot to you.

My clients say:
- I'm grateful for my eyesight.
- I'm grateful for my wife.
- I'm grateful for my writing talent.
- I'm grateful for my education.
- I'm grateful to my current opportunities and more on the way.

Any time you're in a low mood or even feeling a bit frantic, remember to tune into your breath and gratitude. Then you'll be at your best during *10 Seconds to Wealth.*

4)   The Effective 10 Seconds to Inspire Forgiveness When You Made a Mistake

When possible, ask the person, "What makes a real apology to you?"

To get someone to forgive often requires a customized set of actions.

Each person is different. Some people require that you say, "I was wrong."

Others need to see you making amends. You can say, "I was wrong. I want to make this up to you. How can I make amends?"

In my case, I start to feel better when a family member says, "This is my plan so I can avoid making that mistake again."

The *crucial 10 seconds* is when you give the person what

they require so they can start on the path to forgiving you.

What if they won't tell you what they require? Then set up a plan to do these various details:
- say "I was wrong"
- ask "How can I make amends?"
- take action to make amends
- restrain yourself in getting upset if the other person is slow to forgive you (you might need to talk through your anguish with a counselor)

Some teenagers show us exactly what *not* do when it comes to asking for forgiveness. These individuals petulantly say, "I said I was sorry. What do you want from me? How long is this going to go on?"

Instead, it is better to say, "I was wrong. I want to make amends. I'm hoping that you will forgive me when you can."

5) The Effective 10 Seconds to Enhance Your Romantic Relationship

Here's something that will really help your romantic relationship. At some time when things are comfortable between you and your sweetie, ask, "When was a time that I did something that helped you feel really special?"

Listen carefully. When possible, write down some notes. Notice what made the difference. Was it a gift? Just snuggling together watching a sit-com? Helping with your loved one's first novel?

In his book *The 5 Love Languages,* Dr. Gary Chapman identified five different ways (or languages) that mean love to different individuals:
1. Words of Affirmation
2. Quality Time

3. Receiving Gifts

4. Acts of Service

5. Physical Touch (including hugs, neck massages and holding hands)

Each person is different. Although we may all like some of the above items, we tend to have a favorite. Think about it. If you grew up in a house in which chicken soup was an expression of love, it does not matter how much lasagna your sweetie makes for you. So the plan is to discover what means most to your sweetie.

Here's the secret: When you put *10 seconds* into something that really means something to your sweetie, you will truly enhance your relationship.

Book Four:
Prepare Yourself to Be Strong for the Unknowns

Some time ago, a college student in one of my Designing Careers classes, asked, "What one thing do you want us to learn in this class?"

I replied, **"You need preparation to be strong to face the unknowns."**

At times, life can be truly hard on each individual.

Several years ago, someone asked Steven Spielberg, "How do you prepare to direct a feature film?"

"Go to the gym," Spielberg replied. His point being that we need physical endurance to do tough projects like directing a feature film.

I take Spielberg's point literally and I exercise everyday.

In this section, we'll cover material about preparation and principles to make you stronger and help you take effective action.

Here are the topics:
1) Focus and Take Action
2) Nurture Relationships

3) Take Action So You Access the Subconscious Mind to Help You Make Good Changes
4) Develop Discipline to Improve Your Life
5) Use Momentum
6) Nurture Yourself and Give Yourself Compassion
7) Let Go of What's Not Working

1) Focus and Take Action

Here are some principles or secrets of wealth building.

How Ross Perot became a billionaire in eight years ...

Secret 1: Be courageous. Ross Perot had the courage to start his own company, EDS (Electronic Data Systems), and take on IBM—where he had been fired. To sell EDS' services, Ross and other former IBM salespeople approached the same clients they would have contacted when they worked for IBM. Ross began with only $1,000 in savings. The second gutsy thing he did was to give guarantees. EDS would estimate upfront how much it would cost to handle all of the client's data processing needs. Ross assured them that his services would be cheaper than if the client did it themselves internally. EDS would not deviate from their estimate to the client. This was courageous because companies avoid making ironclad estimates since projects often get extended and unknown problems rise up.

Secret 2: Be persistent. It took Ross 78 attempts (from his list of 110 companies) until he made his first deal. At that time, IBM formed a group of five people to start a whispering campaign against EDS. In another gutsy move, Ross hired one of the whispering campaign guys right out from under IBM.

Secret 3: Focus on reusable technology. EDS' data processing programs were usable (with minimal modifications) from state to state, especially when Medicare and Medicaid were beginning in numerous organizations. Ross' use of technology relates to: "Technology is always going to be a source for wealth" (said Mark Victor Hansen, co-creator of the *Chicken Soup for the Soul* series).

Secret 4: Motivate salespeople by giving them stock options. Ross' team of salespeople had a definite stake in the success of the company! As the company does better, the stock options rise in value. For example, Microsoft stock options rose in value, and many founding employees of Microsoft became millionaires.

Secret 5: Make a public offering. At the time, technology companies were offering stocks at 100 times current earnings. EDS' stock was at 14 cents per share, and it was offered at 118 times that amount—totaling $16.50 a share. After the public offering quickly sold out, Ross pocketed $5 million. His remaining shares totaled $154 million—a great return after only six years since being a disgruntled IBM salesman. Ross was 38 years old. Just two years later his shares were worth about $1.4 billion.

That's how Ross Perot became a billionaire in eight years. Ross Perot was certainly skillful as a salesman which helped him land contracts for his company EDS.

Identify your highest skill and devote your time to performing it. Delegate all other skills. – Ronald Brown

2) Nurture Relationships

Many of the best successes were accomplished by teams. Some authors observe that the grand success of Pixar relied all three leaders of the company:
- Steve Jobs (persistence, financial investment, vision and courage to make the audacious move to go public when only *Toy Story* had been completed and released)

- Ed Catmull (leadership and management skill)
- John Lasseter (animation and storytelling skill)

The Walt Disney Company relied on the two brothers/partners:
- Walt Disney (creativity and leadership)
- Roy O. Disney (financial skills)

Many hands, hearts and minds generally contribute to anyone's notable achievement. – Walt Disney

In my college level Designing Careers classes, I emphasize: "Know your tendencies and compensate for them."

My point is to "strengthen your strengths"—that is, focus on raising your skills to world class level. And when necessary, team up with others. We do not need to try to be great at many things. Why? We can team up with others and then observe how projects become *better* than our first imaginings. Collaboration can yield extraordinary results.

Success in show business depends on your ability to make and keep friends. – Sophie Tucker

3) Take Action So You Access the Subconscious Mind to Help You Make Good Changes

In decades of coaching clients and graduate students, I've learned that merely understanding something on the intellectual level often does not create the needed change.

Instead, we need to impact our subconscious mind.

One useful technique is the *Replace Inky Water Method*.

The Replace Inky Water Method

Imagine you have bucket filled with water that is mixed with black ink.

If you pour enough fresh water into the bucket the inky

water will flow out, leaving you with just fresh clear water.

We need words, body posture and music to make sure we flush out old destructive patterns (the inky water).

* * *

Here's how the Replace Inky Water Method works for Sam. Over the years, to feel safe, Sam has adopted the behavior-patterns and thoughts of a perfectionist. Researchers have noted that beneath perfectionism is fear.

Now, he needs more than words to help him calm down.

First, he finds soothing music that he prefers.

Second, he identifies valuable ideas that he wants to make part of himself. He uses one of my phrases: "It's not about perfection; it's about putting one foot in front of the other." He also uses the phrase: "I am safe as I am."

Third, he applies these words to fit like lyrics to his favorite music.

Fourth, he learns to deep breathe—extending his belly as he breathes in and contracting his belly as he breathes out.

Fifth, he places a small pillow behind his back while he is seated. This helps him sit up straight with his vertebrae aligned.

This above combination of techniques helps Sam develop the "space" to make new choices.

Instead of reacting with anger (with the subliminal fear), he can slow down and make better choices. He can choose to respond by writing down the tasks-to-do in his pocket calendar. He can write them on a "holding pattern" list. That is, he can comfort himself by knowing that he has captured the task, and he will place it in his schedule, as appropriate.

The point here is: new ideas need to become part of the person.

The use of words plus music helps the new ideas "fill up the bucket" of the mind. We tend to only focus on one thing at a time. Set a new pattern of focusing on empowering thoughts and feelings. The truth is that no perfectionist can do "all things to feel safe" all of the time. A sense of safety must develop from within the person—not from a reliance on doing external things perfectly. Another idea that goes with "I am safe as I am" is: "I can handle it." Author Susan Jeffers in her book, *Feel the Fear and Do It Anyway*, discusses the transformational power of the idea "I can handle it." A spiritual phrase is "I can handle it with God."

Here's another example of using the Replace Inky Water Method. My client Marlena wanted to expand her prosperity. She said, "I need to gain more sales. But I'm nervous about making cold phone calls to prospective customers." Using the Replace Inky Water Method, she listens to a favorite, energizing song with the lyrics: "You're Simply the Best!" (sung by Tina Turner). She also holds her arms up in the air like an Olympic Gymnast celebrating a perfect landing. These two details help her flood out her nervousness with a new empowering state of being. The truth is that Marlena has the power to shift her state of being. She immediately dials the next phone number.

This Replace Inky Water Method is a helpful part of waking up our spirit.

The Replace Inky Water Method is more powerful than mere words.

There are only two ways to live your life. One is as though nothing is a miracle. The other is as though everything is a miracle. – Albert Einstein

It is best to use the Replace Inky Water Method so that we remember the miracles in our life. Pause for a moment; remember how wonderful it felt to have your sweetheart in your life—especially at the beginning of your relationship. Remember the feeling of closeness and how grateful you were to be together. And being together now is still a miracle—it is still a blessing. This is the truth. Over time we can come to let the miracle feel like something commonplace.

Refresh your view of the miracles in your life.
That's how we need to approach filling our minds and our emotions. And that's why we choose to use the Replace Inky Water Method.

We can start with words, representing the ideas we want to focus on. Then we need to go to the next level: we need to engage multiple senses—and in this way we are pouring in more fresh water.

Using music is a powerful way to continue.

I like to recall some music by John Barry. His orchestrations immediately place my body at ease. Then, I think of a few words like: "God relaxes Tom." As I listen to the music I even think of the words as lyrics.

Researchers note that people remember lyrics with ease. The combination of words and music flow easily into our long-term memory. Also, our bodies feel differently in response to words and music. This is why creating your own empowering lyrics to your favorite songs is extremely powerful.

Choose songs that build you up. Earlier, I mentioned the song with the lyrics: "You're Simply the Best!" Those words and music can build a person up. The person's state of being changes instantly.

4) Develop Discipline to Improve Your Life
Developing new habits takes discipline.

Discipline is simply sticking to those commitments you make

for yourself, which are made out of a love for your vision.
– Suzanne Falter-Barns

Suzanne Falter-Barns also wrote: "Get a coach or a support buddy to help you with [discipline and things you don't like doing]. Call or e-mail when you're balking at your commitment. If you get the answering machine, tell it that you'll be sitting down to work now, and will call back when the work is complete. Then make the happy call at the end of your work session."

My addition to this idea is something I call *Ease into Momentum*. The idea is to take out the pain. And find something easy you can do to get started. For example, if you want to write a book, start with writing two paragraphs a day. I call this the *Easy Part Start*. You are doing something easy that adds up to great results.

5) Use Momentum

President John F. Kennedy started the process of momentum when he provided a vision and leadership with his proclamation: "I believe this nation should commit itself, before this decade is out, to land a man on the Moon and return him safely to Earth." At the time, there was no fully formed space program.

Leadership entailed setting the goal before figuring out how to get it done.

"This nation has tossed its cap over the wall of space, and we have no choice but to follow it," said President Kennedy. He meant that we have no other choice but to continue the momentum of what we had begun. Similarly, Walt Disney's brother and partner Roy O. Disney said, "Decision-making is easy if your values are clear."

At various times, you will embark on new chapters in life. During these times you might find yourself, like the early space program, to be charting new territory—especially when seeking to get out of a financial rut. What counts is to keep the momentum going.

To really support momentum, use both *Effort-Goals* and *Result-Goals*.

Effort-Goal: This is a goal that you have control over.

Something for which you can choose to devote your energy and effort. For example, a salesperson or business owner can choose the number of phone calls she makes to generate income.

Result-Goal: This is a goal that involves an outcome. However, please note that we cannot control outcomes that are dependent on factors beyond our control like the weather, someone else's mood or how a particular company is doing in the marketplace.

A salesperson says she wants to increase her quarterly sales by 20% (Result-Goal). When she sets up her Effort-Goal of increasing her phone calls by 30%, she can make progress. But she only increases her sales by 10%. She can still feel good about achieving her Effort-Goal of increasing phone calls by 30%.

When you separate Effort-Goals from Result-Goals you can create steady progress and keep up your morale.

We notice that to get a particular Result Goal, like more sales, we can influence the outcome by putting energy into our Effort-Goals. To get more done, here is a principle that I share with audiences: *Keep score and achieve more.*

For example, while writing a book, I note how many words I write in each session (which is how I "keep score"). I turn the process into a game. This ties in with my other favorite principle *Make it a game you can win.*

6) Nurture Yourself and Give Yourself Compassion

I emphasize the value of practicing self-leadership and setting up structure in your life with daily habits of discipline.

We must all suffer from one of two pains: the pain of discipline or the pain of regret. The difference is discipline weighs ounces while regret weighs tons. – Jim Rohn

Still, I realize that we need *personal energy* to take disciplined action. Where does that energy come from? Nurturing yourself.

Compassion for myself is the most powerful healer of them all.
– Dr. Theodore Isaac Rubin

Sometimes the most compassionate thing you can do is to let people in. It can take courage to express some vulnerability (with an appropriate friend or family member).

Trouble is part of your life, and if you don't share it, you don't give the person who loves you a chance to love your enough.
– Dinah Shore

Ask yourself these questions and then write a few things into your calendar: "How can I give to myself? How can I treat myself like I am my own best friend?"

By the way, stop berating yourself!

Here's one way to change your self-talk. Say:

Before now, I did not _____. Today, I am doing ____ and making progress.

Some people make the mistake of berating themselves as if mean-talk will "whip them into shape." No! Demoralizing self-talk merely saps personal energy.

Show compassion for yourself and encourage yourself. And get support whether it's a support group, new friends, quiet time, prayer time, or something else.

Step forward today, showing yourself kindness and flexibility.

7) Let Go of What's Not Working

Bestselling author Erica Jong wrote: "I have not ceased being fearful, but I have ceased to let fear control me." The point is that she let go of what was not working: paralysis due to fear.

Take steps to let go of what's not working. How? First admit that something is holding you back in your life.

Some of the toughest times in my life have been around losing two friends who really stopped being a healthy part of my life. I know for a fact that I now have more energy and feel better now that these two people are not in my life.

But I dragged my feet in letting them go.

One former friend even said to me, "This phone conversation was largely useless."

I had just spent much of the time listening to this guy—as I had done many times over the years.

I replied, "I don't do useless things. So I will not be calling you. If you have an emergency, you can call me. I still care about you. But this is not healthy. I wish you many blessings ..."

I had to actually log each day (in the beginning) to encourage myself to not call this friend who had been part of my life for 30 years.

It's been years since that time, and my life is better now.

To create a life of abundance, step forward and drop the useless baggage as you go.

Useless baggage can be a result of behavior patterns that once garnered praise—perhaps during childhood. For example, in her book *Nice Girls Don't Get Rich*, Lois P. Frankel expresses the premise that effective women drop the behavior patterns of "nice little girls"—that were instilled by parents and guardians. Effective women learn to be assertive and take care of finances. In this example, we can view the nice girls' behavior patterns as useless baggage.

Things to let go:
- Going into debt merely for consumer toys.
- Resentment over past mistakes.
- As a reflex, reaching for something that costs money to serve as an emotional bandage.

One Way to Let Go of What's Not Working: Seek Wisdom and Apply It to Your Life

I've invited some learned people to share insights in this book.

We'll begin by learning from Mike Robbins' insights about working with fear that may arise.

*****GUEST ARTICLE BELOW*****
How to Move Through Fear
by Mike Robbins

Fear is something that we all experience, especially on our journey toward deeper authenticity, fulfillment, and success in life. Being who we really are, expressing ourselves boldly, and going for what we want in life can cause a great deal of fear in us.

I get scared all the time—especially when I'm taking risks, doing new things, and putting myself out there. When I was younger I thought there was something really wrong with me because I would get so nervous—in sports, in school, in social settings, and more. I now understand that everyone else experiences their own version of the same basic fears I have (being judged, making mistakes, looking bad, failing, disappointing others, and more). It's just part of being human.

Many of us run away or hide from our fears because they seem scary, uncomfortable, or embarrassing. We also erroneously think we "shouldn't" have them or we're somehow "wrong" for feeling scared. However, most things that mean a lot to us in life don't show up without any fear at all. And as we strive to live with authenticity, it's inevitable that we'll get scared along the way.

The question isn't whether or not we experience fear in our lives (because we all do and always will for as long as we live); the more important question for each of us to ask and answer is, how can I move through my fears in an honest way so they don't stop me from being who I really am and going for what I truly want in life?

How to Move Through Your Fear in a Positive Way

1) Admit it—Acknowledge your fear, tell the truth about it, and be real. When we feel scared and are willing to admit it with a sense of empathy and compassion for ourselves, it can often take the edge off and give us a little breathing room to begin with.

2) Own it—Take responsibility for your fear and own it as yours, not anyone else's. We often have a tendency to blame others for doing or saying things that "scare" us. However, when we remember that no one else can "make" us scared—only we have that power—we take back the responsibility and the power of the fear and remember that it exists within us, so we are the only ones who can change it.

3) Feel it—Allow yourself to feel your fear, not just think about it or talk about it (something I often catch myself doing). Feel it in your body and allow yourself to go into the emotion of it, even if it is scary or uncomfortable. Like any emotion, when we feel our fear deeply and passionately, it has a way of dissipating.

4) Express it—Let it out. Speak, write, emote, move your body, yell, or do whatever you feel is necessary for you to do to express your fear. Similar to feeling any emotion with intensity, when we express emotions with intensity and passion, they move right through us. When we repress our emotions, they get stuck and can become debilitating and dangerous.

5) Let it go—This one is often easier said than done—for me and many people I work with. Letting go of our fear becomes much easier when we honestly admit, own, feel, and express it. Letting go of our fear is a conscious and deliberate choice, not a reactionary form of denial. Once you've allowed yourself the time to work through your fear, you can declare "I'm choosing to let go of my fear and use its energy in a positive way."

6) Visualize the positive outcomes you desire—Think about, speak out loud, write down, or even close your eyes and visualize how you want things to be and, more important, how you want to feel. If your fear is focused on something specific like your work, a relationship, money, etc.—visualize it being how you want it to be and allow yourself to feel how you ultimately want to feel.

7) Take action—Be willing to take bold and courageous actions, even if you're still feeling nervous. Your legs may shake, your voice might quiver, but that doesn't have to stop you from saying what's on your mind, taking a risk, making a request, trying something new, or being bold in a small or big way. Doing this is what builds confidence and allow us to move through our fear.

Fear can and does stop us in life—from being ourselves, speaking our truth, and going for what we really want. But, when we remember with compassion that there's nothing wrong with us for getting scared and when we're willing to lean into our fears with vulnerability and boldness—we can literally transform them into something that catapults our growth and fulfillment in life.

Mike Robbins is the author of three books, *Focus on the Good Stuff; Be Yourself, Everyone Else is Already Taken;* and *Nothing Changes Until You Do*. As an expert in teamwork, emotional intelligence, and the powers of appreciation and authenticity, Mike delivers keynote addresses and customized seminars that empower people, teams, and organizations to work together effectively and be more successful. He has inspired tens of thousands of people around the world to reach new levels of awareness and productivity, both personally and professionally. Through his speeches, seminars, and writing, Mike teaches people important techniques that allow them to be more grateful, appreciative, and authentic with others and themselves.

His clients include Google, Wells Fargo, Adobe, Charles Schwab, Twitter, the U.S. Department of Labor, Gap, New York Life, Stanford University, Chevron, eBay, Kaiser, UC Berkeley, Genentech, the San Francisco Giants, and many others. Mike is a member of the National Speakers Association. He has been featured on ABC News, the Oprah radio network, in *Forbes*, the *Washington Post*, and many others. He is a regular contributor to Oprah.com and the Huffington Post. In addition to his three books, Mike is also a contributing author to: *Chicken Soup for the Single Parent's Soul, Creating a Marriage You'll Love,* and *Thirty Things to Do When You Turn Thirty*.

Reach Mike at www.mike-robbins.com

* * *

Now Dr. Arthur Ciaramicoli shares methods for turning our thoughts and feelings in a positive direction.

*****GUEST ARTICLE BELOW*****

How to be Positive in a Negative World
by Dr. Arthur P. Ciaramicoli

When I was a young boy my father gave me Norman

Vincent Peale's book *The Power of Positive Thinking* and told me that after I finished the book I could move a tree if I believed I could. I read parts of the book and was admittedly a bit puzzled. I understood the point about being positive but didn't quite understand how I could actually make myself think positive and move mountains. The instruction book seemed to be missing although I liked the concept.

In today's culture we are bombarded with self help books, motivational speakers and CD's providing instructions of how to be and remain positive. I don't think anyone denies the value of being positive but most of us who follow the simple instructions aren't quite able to maintain this positive state as easily as we are instructed.

What is the missing ingredient?

Awareness of Your Story

Negativity is almost always based on inaccurate interpretations of reality. One of my group therapy clients joined our sessions due to being overly stressed and struggling with self consciousness about his self image. Two aspects of his life embarrassed him greatly, the blue collar town he grew up in and the so-called mediocre college he attended. Over time he let us know of his embarrassment. After several months of sessions, he has learned that his perception of his inferiority was a distorted view he needlessly carried with him for several years. As he unraveled his negative story so did others.

One woman talked of not being pretty enough, we determined this perception was not true. Another woman thought she didn't speak well, not true. A few of the men talked of thinking their balding hairlines make them unattractive, not true. One man talked of his superior intelligence, also not true. Whether distortions about oneself are positive or negative the truth must be discerned in order to remain positive in life. You can't be positive with consistency if you're not dealing with reality. The foundation of your sense of self has to be solid and stable. Distortions create road maps that take us to the wrong destination with the wrong people.

Over the years of doing group sessions I have heard these types of stories over and over again. The emotional distress of negative thinking is profound and if you don't become aware of where your biases originated you are doomed to continue living in the prison of pessimism.

The Truth Expands our Vision

Knowing the truth about who you are is a process that can't occur quickly or without significant effort. Just trying to think positively won't work for long if your old story is embedded in your psyche. It takes time, patience and persistence to change negative views to more realistic perspectives.

First we must become aware of our biases; of course we need other objective rational people to help us come to accurate conclusions about ourselves. Then the hard work begins. We have to change the view we established early in life for the new view we have come to learn as adults. We were quite impressionable as young people; taking in the views of others later in life is not easy even if the feedback we are receiving is complimentary. It takes time and trust to come to believe that the negative views we held about ourselves may have originated through our relationships with biased caretakers, coaches, teachers and other significant authority figures as well as peers.

Eventually, with courage and determination, the new view replaces the old negativity and we are finally in a position to live our lives with a positive, realistic view of ourselves. The truth has freed us from the past once we integrate new information in our heart and mind. I emphasize heart as many of us know that our negativity is not rational but it persists as it is recorded deep in the emotional parts of the brain. Change means we have to re-arrange ourselves emotionally as well as intellectually, which is why it never occurs quickly or easily. We can understand without changing. Change has to be an active process involving behavior, intellect and emotion.

Once we have done this work the negativity in our environment and in the world has far less impact on our outlook. When we are at peace within we can tolerate the chaos around us without being effected in major ways. We have reached a state of calm allowing us to tolerate the stress outside of us without becoming overly stressed ourselves. We have then become models for balanced living.

Arthur P. Ciaramicoli, Ed.D., Ph.D., is a licensed clinical psychologist and member of the American Psychological Association. Dr. Ciaramicoli has been on the faculty of Harvard Medical School for several years, lecturer for the American Cancer Society, Chief Psychologist at Metrowest Medical Center, and director of the Metrowest Counseling Center. Dr. Ciaramicoli has lectured at Harvard Health Services, Boston College Counseling Center, the Space Telescope Science Institute as well as being a consultant to several major corporations. Dr. Ciaramicoli is a seasoned media expert, appearing on CNN, CNNfn, Fox News Boston, Comcast TV, New England Cable News, Good Morning America Weekend, The O'Reilly Report, and other shows. Dr. Ciaramicoli is the author of *The Curse of the Capable: The Hidden Challenges to a Balanced, Healthy, High Achieving Life; Performance Addiction: The Dangerous New Syndrome and How to Stop It from Ruining Your Life;* and *The Stress Solution*.

His newsletter, blog comments and contact information are available at his web site, BalanceYourSuccess.com

* * *

Now, Dr. Elayne Savage shares insights about stretching, trying new actions and reaping the rewards.

*****GUEST ARTICLE BELOW*****

Self-Acceptance, Self-Respect, and Self-Appreciation
by Elayne Savage, Ph.D.

I'm so proud of my accomplishment. I just assembled four IKEA storage units. By myself.

And I didn't listen to the nay-sayers:

"You won't be able to do it without help."

"No way. It's too difficult."

"The directions are so confusing. Only drawings, no words."

"You'll get frustrated and give up before it's done."

My response was to stubbornly insist *I can do this!*

For a change I didn't buy into those old messages that in the past would have paralyzed me:

"Who do you think you are?"

"What makes you think you can do this?"

I just knew I could do the assembly. How? I was remembering another time when everyone warned me I wouldn't be able to do something.

I was eleven years old. Uncle Max gave me a headlamp for my bicycle. I was so excited when I opened the package, expecting to find a headlight. Then I saw many parts lying there, looking nothing like the picture on the box.

My dad offered to assemble it for me. Days turned into weeks. I kept asking "When?" He kept saying, "Soon."

Soon never happened. Each month that went by was another disappointment. I gave up on my dad.

I was determined to get that headlight mounted on my handlebars. I decided to put it together myself. Yes, I struggled with it. Yes, I made mistakes.

Eventually I got that headlamp up and working. My childhood success with that headlamp let me take on the IKEA challenge. I was able to tap into that childhood success and to trust it.

What's a Mistake or Three?

I did make some mistakes. More than once I had to disassemble my work and reassemble it. By the time I got to the second unit, I learned from my mistakes. I'm grateful I was able to tap into a long ago memory of an ability to put things together. I'm grateful to call up the ability to trust myself enough to attempt this project. I'm grateful that I could allow myself to make mistakes and not judge myself harshly. I'm grateful that I can let myself be proud of my accomplishment.

I'm grateful for the chance to experience self-acceptance, self-respect, and self-appreciation.

Lessons From the Yellow Submarine

Another way of transforming abilities is to practice borrowing from one compartment within yourself and move it to another.

Can you visualize a hallway with rooms on either side? Do you remember the scene in *The Yellow Submarine* cartoon movie? Remember how the Beatles characters were running back and forth across the hall from room to room?

Imagine that a room contains skills you developed in childhood and adolescence.

Think of this room as a storage area, with every possible type of storage container.

Can you imagine yourself rummaging through these early strengths that have been tucked away? Can you imagine selecting one or two? You can take your time as you let the process of choosing, sorting, and selecting unfold.

Then gather up this new energy you have found. Carry it across the hall to another room, another compartment, another part of yourself. Take it to a place where you have the space to appreciate your skills in a new way.

Consider ways you can recognize skills that exist in one area of your life and transfer them to another area. In this new space you have created, you might find this new energy begins to transform into something even more precious and useful.

Transforming Self-Rejection into Self-Acceptance

However, for some of us, recognizing and appreciating our abilities is not always easy. Some of us somehow missed out on the essential building blocks of childhood—things like self-esteem, self-assurance, or social skills.

Sometimes it seems that we only have stumbling blocks instead of building blocks.

I can also recall some experiences even earlier than the headlamp adventure. I can recall having real-life building blocks as a young child: my erector set. Perhaps some of you had building blocks as well. Maybe wooden alphabet blocks or Lincoln Logs or Legos.

Did you have a favorite? What was it? Can you picture the pieces now?

Visualize taking them down from the shelf and spreading them around you on a table or the floor.

Can you imagine what they felt like in your hands?

How did you put them together?

What was your step-by-step process of building?

What can you learn from recalling your building process?

Can you transfer these skills over to how you approach tasks and problems today? Instead of undermining, you can practice bolstering, reinforcing, fortifying, buttressing, bracing, or shoring up your resources.

For me, the most wondrous transformation of all is the process of transforming self-rejection into self-acceptance. Successfully putting together those IKEA storage units was an important step for me along the road of self-acceptance, self-respect, and self-appreciation.

Elayne Savage, Ph.D., The Queen of Rejection,® is a communication coach and expert on taking things personally and the fear of rejection. A professional member of the National Speakers Association, she is a workshop leader, trainer, and consultant. Her relationship books, *Breathing Room—Creating Space to Be a Couple* and *Don't Take It Personally! The Art of Dealing with Rejection* have been published in 9 languages.

510-540-6230

elayne@QueenofRejection.com

www.QueenofRejection.com

* * *

As I mentioned above, you can feel empowered to let go of what's not working when *you seek the wisdom of learned people and apply that wisdom to your life.*

So make space for better people, opportunities and resources. How? Let go of what's not working.

* * *

This section has been about strengthening yourself. When you're stronger and more poised, you will do much better during the *10 Seconds to Wealth.*

One final crucial point: **Happiness and success often**

arise when we serve well.

Happiness is not a goal; it is a by-product. – Eleanor Roosevelt
Work is love made visible. - Kahil Gibran
It is faith in something and enthusiasm for something that makes life worth living. - Oliver Wendell Holmes
I don't know what your destiny will be, but one thing I know: the only ones among you who will be really happy are those who will have sought and found how to serve. – Albert Schweitzer

I invite you to look for and *discover* how you can serve well other people and enjoy using your skills and talents.

The best to you.

In Summary:
Here are the 12 Principles in Context:
Jan. – New Beginnings
Principle #1: Share in your Divine Gifts.

Feb. – Valentine's Day; Approach the Moment with Love
Principle #2: Uplift through "the most important"

Mar. – March 4th ("March forth")
Principle #3: Concentrate on Top Six Targets

Apr. – April Showers
Principle #4: Create your "reserves."

May – May the Force Be With You
Principle #5: Energize "10 Seconds to Wealth"

June – June Weddings
Principle #6: Succeed through commitment to "the pipeline and better-than-zero"

July – 4th of July
Principle #7: Sort and Declare a New Chapter of Life.

Aug. – Friendship Day
Principle #8: Act to support friendships.

Sept. – Back to School
Principle #9: Continue learning.

Oct. – Halloween
Principle #10: Target "act it until you become it."

Nov. – Thanksgiving
Principle #11: Nurture gratitude.

Dec. – Holiday Season
Principle #12: Open with "the sacred."

BONUS Principle: Win by Listening.

A FINAL WORD AND THE SPRINGBOARD TO YOUR DREAMS

Congratulations on your efforts as your worked with the material in this book. To get even more value from this book, take the plans and insights that you created and place them in some form in your calendar or day planner. *Plan and take action.* Return to these pages again and again to reconnect with the material and take your life to higher levels.

The best to you,

Tom

Tom Marcoux

Executive Coach and Spoken Word Strategist

Special Offer Just for Readers of this Book:

Contact Tom Marcoux at tomsupercoach@gmail.com for special discounts on **coaching**, books, workshops and presentations. Just mention your experience with this book.

Excerpt from
Darkest Secrets of Persuasion and Seduction Masters: How to Protect Yourself and Turn the Power to Good
by Tom Marcoux, Executive Coach – Spoken Word Strategist
Copyright Tom Marcoux

... Now, I am in my 40's, with gray in my hair, and for 27 years I have been taking action to protect people.

And now is the time for me to protect you with the Countermeasures I reveal in this book.

Every human being needs to be able to break the trance that a Manipulator creates. You need to make good decisions so you are safe and you keep growing—and you are not cut down and crippled.

This Darkest Secrets material is so intense that I first released it only with the counterbalance of my most energizing and uplifting books, Nothing Can Stop You This Year! and 10 Seconds to Wealth: Master the Moment Using Your Divine Gifts.

An interviewer asked me: "Who can be the Manipulator?"

A co-worker, a boss, a salesperson, someone you're

dating, and someone you think is a friend.

Now is the time—this very minute—for me to write this book to protect you.

I must speak the truth.

These Darkest Secrets of "persuasion masters" are ...

Wait a minute! Let's say it plainly: These are the Darkest Secrets of masters of manipulation. Throughout this book, I will call these people what they are: Manipulators.

Dictionary.com defines "manipulate" as "To influence or manage shrewdly or deviously.... To tamper with or falsify for personal gain."

In this book, we will look on a manipulator as one who deviously influences someone with no concern about that person's well-being, and who causes harm to that person.

Here is the first Darkest Secret:

Darkest Secret #1:
Manipulators Make You Hurt
and Then Offer the Salve.

Manipulators would invite you to go out in the sun for hours and then sell you the salve to soothe your burns. The problem is that we don't notice that this is what they're doing.

For example, you're considering the purchase of a house. A Manipulator asks the question, "So, where would you put your TV?" This question is designed to put you into a trance.

Dictionary.com defines "trance" as "a half-conscious state, seemingly between sleeping and waking, in which ability to function voluntarily may be suspended." Let's condense this: in a trance you may not be able to function freely.

Here is the second Secret:

Darkest Secret #2:
Manipulators Put You into a Trance.

To protect yourself, you must learn to use Countermeasures to Break the Trance.

All the Countermeasures (actions you can take to break the trance) in this book will make you stronger and more capable of protecting yourself.

Now, we'll view the third Secret:

Darkest Secret #3:

Manipulators Care Nothing for You and Human Decency: They'll lie, cheat, and do whatever they need to do so they win—but their charm masks all this.

Let's return to the example of a Manipulator selling you a house. A Manipulator does not pause for an instant to see if you can truly afford the new house. The Manipulator would neglect to mention that you will not only have your mortgage payment of $900. There will be additional costs: home repairs, property tax, water, electricity, homeowner's insurance, and more. The Manipulator only emphasizes what he or she knows you want to hear: "Look! $900 is better than the $1500 you're paying for rent, which is just going down the toilet. And the $900 is an investment."

Let's go back to **Darkest Secret #1:**

Manipulators make you hurt and then offer the salve.

The Manipulator has you feeling good about the solution (salve) and feeling bad about your current life situation.

How? A Manipulator will make you hurt through questions such as:

- What bothers you about paying $1500 a month for rent? (The Manipulator will use a derisive tone when he says the word rent.)
- What is not smart about paying rent on someone else's house instead of investing in your own house?
- How do you feel about your children walking in the neighborhood where you live now?

Do you see how these questions are designed to make you hurt enough so that you'll buy?

An interviewer asked me, "Tom, aren't these good arguments for purchasing a house?"

"What we're looking at is the *intention* of the influencer," I replied. "Let's look at our definition of a manipulator as one who deviously influences someone with no concern about that person's well-being, and who causes harm to that person. If the person truly cannot afford the house, he or she will be harmed by buying it. If the manipulator conceals the truth, the manipulator is doing harm. That's the important difference."

Some friends of mine are ethical and helpful real estate agents who truthfully reveal the whole situation and help the purchaser achieve her own goals.

In this book, we are talking about another type of person; that is, unethical Manipulators.

* * *

In any given moment, we need to remember the tactics Manipulators use. We will focus on the word D.A.R.K. so you can remember details easily and protect yourself from Manipulators.

D — Dangle something for nothing
A — Alert to scarcity
R — Reveal the Desperate Hot Button
K — Keep on pushing buttons

1. Dangle Something for Nothing

What do conmen and conwomen do to seize your attention? They make you think you're getting a "steal."

I recently saw a documentary in which a conman on a street in England showed a toy that looked like it was dancing. This fake product was actually dancing because of a hidden, invisible thread. The conman was dangling something for nothing. The Entranced Buyer thought he was getting something worth $20 for only $5. That was the trick. The Entranced Buyer felt that he was getting $15 extra of value for his $5. What the Buyer really got was something worth nothing. Similarly, I know someone who purchased a copy of a Disney movie from a street vendor in San Francisco. She brought the copy home and it was unwatchable—and the street vendor was never seen again.

An old phrase goes, "A conman cannot con someone who is not looking for something for nothing."

How to Protect Yourself from "Dangle Something for Nothing"

Stop! Get on your cell phone and talk through the "deal" with someone you know who thinks clearly. Go home. Think about it. Do some research on the Internet. Listen to your gut feelings. If the salesman or conman is too insistent, get away from that Manipulator. Get quiet. Have a cup of water. Cool down. Break the Trance!

Break the Trance and Identify the Crucial Detail

Earlier, I mentioned that a Manipulator puts you into a trance. An added problem is that we put ourselves into a trance. For example, as you read this, are you thinking about your right toe? Most likely not (unless you stubbed your toe recently). The point is that we only focus on a tiny percentage of what is going on in our life.

Around fifteen years ago, I caused myself trouble because I put myself into a trance. I discovered that under certain conditions, friendship can make you nearly deaf. Here's how: I was producing a song for a motion picture. A good friend was singing backup in the chorus. Because of our friendship, I wanted him to sound great. I completely missed the Crucial Detail. In this kind of situation, the Crucial Detail is that what truly counts is how the lead singer sounds! I made a song that I could not release. What a waste of time and money! I had put myself into a trance.

In any situation in which the Manipulator is "dangling something for nothing," we often fall into a trance and miss the Crucial Detail. The most important detail is *not* that we're saving money if we order before midnight tonight. What counts is whether the product creates a lasting, crucial benefit in our lives. And is the benefit of the product worth the cost? Some people even program themselves to make mistakes by saying, "I can't pass up a bargain." The bargain is *not* the Crucial Detail.

Secrets to Break the Trance

This is the process of B.R.E.A.K.S. It will help you remember the proven methods to break a trance.

B — Breathe
R — Relax
E — Envision
A — Act on aromas
K — Keep moving
S — Smile

Secret #1: Breathe

Remember Secret #1: Manipulators make you hurt and then offer the salve. The Manipulator wants to put you into a state of being that fills you with a sense of urgency and anxiety. Oh, no! I'm going to miss the sale!

Stop this highly vulnerable state. Take a deep breath.
End of Excerpt from
Darkest Secrets of Persuasion and Seduction Masters: How to Protect Yourself and Turn the Power to Good

Purchase your copy of this book (paperback or eBook) at Amazon.com or BarnesandNoble.com

See **Free Chapters** of Tom Marcoux's 40 books at http://amzn.to/ZiCTRj

ABOUT THE AUTHOR

You want more and better, right? Imagine fulfilling your Big Dream.

Tom Marcoux can help you—in that he's coached thousands of people: CEOs, small business leaders, graduate students (at Stanford University) speakers, and authors.

Marcoux is known as an effective **Executive Coach** and **Spoken Word Strategist.**

(and Thought Leader—okay, writing 40 books helped with that!)

** *CEOs, Vice-Presidents, Other Executives, Small Business Leaders:*

You know that leading people and speaking at your best can be tough.

Marcoux solves problems while helping you amplify your own Charisma, Confidence and Control of Time.

Interested? Email Marcoux—tomsupercoach@gmail.com

Ask for a *Special Report:*

* 9 Deadly Mistakes to Avoid for Your Next Speech

** *Speakers, Experts—for a great TED Talk, Book, Audio Book, Speeches, YouTube Videos.*

Marcoux solve problems while helping you to make your Concise, Compelling Message that gets people to trust you and get what you're offering (product, service, *an idea*).

Yes—the *San Francisco Examiner* designated Tom Marcoux as "The Personal Branding Instructor."

Marcoux is an expert on STORY. He won a Special Award at the EMMY AWARDS, and he directed a feature film that went to the CANNES FILM MARKET and earned international distribution.

(Marcoux helps you *be heard and be trusted*—a focus point of his 16th Anniversary edition book, *Connect: High Trust Communication for Your Success in Business and Life*.)

As a CEO, Marcoux leads teams in the United Kingdom, India and the USA. Marcoux guides clients & audiences (IBM, Sun Microsystems, etc.) in leadership, team-building, power time management and branding. See Tom's Popular BLOG: www.TomSuperCoach.com

Specialties: coach to CEOS * Executives * Small Business owners * Leaders * Speakers * Experts * Authors * Academics

One of his *Darkest Secrets* books rose to #1 on Amazon.com Hot New Releases in Business Life (and in Business Communication). A member of the National Speakers Association for over 15 years, Marcoux is a professional coach and guest expert on TV, radio, and print.

Marcoux addressed National Association of Broadcasters' Conference six years running. With a degree in psychology, he is a guest lecturer at **Stanford University**, DeAnza, & California State University, and teaches business communication, designing careers, public speaking, science fiction cinema/literature and comparative religion at Academy of Art University. He is engaged in book/film projects *Crystal Pegasus* (children's) and *Jack AngelSword* (thriller-fantasy). See Tom's well-received blogs

at www.BeHeardandBeTrusted.com

at www.YourBodySoulandProsperity.com

Consider engaging **Tom Marcoux as your Executive Coach.**

"As Tom's client for many years, I have benefited from his wisdom and strategic approach. Do your career and personal life a big favor and get his books and engage him as **your Executive Coach**." – Dr. JoAnn Dahlkoetter, author of *Your Performing Edge* and Coach to CEOs and Olympic Gold Medalists

"Tom Marcoux coached me to get more done in 10 days than other coaches in 2 years." – Brad Carlson, CEO of MindStrong LLC

As the Spoken Word Strategist, Tom Marcoux can help you with **speech writing** and **coaching for your best performance.**

As Tom says, *Make Your Speech a Pleasant Beach.*

Join Tom's Linkedin.com group: *Executive Public Speaking and Communication Power.*

At Google+: join the community "Create Your Best Life – Charisma & Confidence"

Get a **Free** report: "9 Deadly Mistakes to Avoid for Your Next Speech and 9 Surefire Methods" at
http://tomsupercoach.com/freereport9Mistakes4Speech.html

Tom Marcoux has trained CEOs, small business owners, and graduate students to speak with impact and gain audiences' tremendous approval and cooperation. *Learn how to present and get thunderous applause!*

"Tom, Thanks for your coaching and work with me on revising my speech at a major university. Working with you has been so enlightening for me. Through your gentle prodding and guidance, I was able to write a speech that connects with the audience. I wish everyone could experience the transformation I have undergone. You have helped me discover the warm and compelling stories that now make my speech reach hearts and uplift minds. This was truly an empowering experience. I cannot thank you enough for your great assistance." — J.S.

- **"Tom Marcoux has been an NAB Conference favorite [speaker] for six years. And he is very energetic."** – John Marino, Vice President, National Assn. of Broadcasters, Washington, D.C.

- "Using just one of Tom Marcoux's methods, I got more done in 2 weeks than in 6 months." – Jaclyn Freitas, M.A.

Tom's Coaching features innovations:
- Dynamic Rehearsal
- Power Rehearsal for Crisis
- The Charisma Advantage that Saves You Time

Become a fan of Tom's graphic novels/feature films:
- Fantasy Thriller: *Jack AngelSword*
  type "JackAngelSword" at Facebook.com
- Science fiction: *TimePulse*
  www.facebook.com/timepulsegraphicnovel
- Children's Fantasy: *Crystal Pegasus*
  www.facebook.com/crystalpegasusandrose

See **Free Chapters** of Tom Marcoux's 40 books at http://amzn.to/ZiCTRj   Amazon.com

www.ingramcontent.com/pod-product-compliance
Lightning Source LLC
Chambersburg PA
CBHW060524100426
42743CB00009B/1420